TRUST
IN
TRANSITION

Navigating Organizational Change

Bob Whipple

Photo credits: Photo by Eric Stella for the Barcore. Styling by Luis Santiago Collazo for The Creative Mind-Media and Style Group. Photo used with permission.

ASTD Press is an internationally renowned source of insightful and practical information on workplace learning, performance, and professional development.

ASTD Press
1640 King Street Box 1443
Alexandria, VA 22313-1443 USA

Ordering information: Books published by ASTD Press can be purchased by visiting ASTD's website at store.astd.org or by calling 800.628.2783 or 703.683.8100.

Library of Congress Control Number: 2014944607

ISBN-10: 1-56286-924-8
ISBN-13: 978-1-56286-924-3
e-ISBN: 978-1-60728-428-4

ASTD Press Editorial Staff:
Director: Glenn Saltzman
Manager, ASTD Press: Ashley McDonald
Associate Editor: Sarah Cough
Community of Practice Manager, Management: Ron Lippock
Editorial Assistant: Ashley Slade
Text and Cover Design: Marisa Kelly

Printed by Versa Press, Inc., East Peoria, IL, www.versapress.com.

Contents

Contents

Part V: The Games People Play

Part VI: Wrap Up

Acknowledgments

I thank Bob Vanourek and Don Strickland for their comments on an early draft of this book. Your ideas and suggestions have made the work significantly more user-friendly and more technically competent.

Also, I thank my wife, Kay, who has been my rock through this process, once again. Having a life partner who freely gives so much to help my business on a continual basis is inspiring. I am blessed.

Part I:
Organizations Change

This book about organizational change presents a new conceptual framework and strategy that will enable smoother transitions. Unlike many other books on change, this work advocates a holistic approach that considers the impact on all stakeholders.

Introduction

Trust in Transition was written for professionals who need to navigate organizational change and will be most helpful to the people who lead these efforts. Leaders who heed the advice in this book will improve all aspects of any major change initiative.

The following chapters cover all kinds of change, including minor changes in reporting relationships, changes in job scope, and reorganization efforts—from department consolidations to major upheavals like mergers and acquisitions. The issues are similar regardless of the magnitude. Most organizational changes are attempts to pool strengths and eventually drive costs down to improve competitive positioning. Normally envisioned as a way to ensure survival, change efforts often lead to chaos and even to extinction.

One root cause of failure is when top leaders focus too much energy on the mechanical and financial aspects of the consolidation and not enough on the cultural integration. The solution is to begin the cultural integration work at the same time that the mechanical aspects are being considered, and to staff the cultural effort for success. A central thesis of this book is that the culture determines the effectiveness of an organization at all times.

Every day organizations announce changes and expect, or at least hope, that people will react positively to them. How leaders manage a transition has everything to do with how successful it will be. Any reorganization is likely to fail unless the cultures can be made to mesh well.

Business leaders are smart people, but their attention has been directed so strongly toward the physical, financial, and mechanical aspects of organizational change that they miss the boat on the cultural aspects until they are too far into the process. The root cause of the high failure rate for reorganizations is that people are often left out of the equation, or there is little consideration for how they will be affected by the move. This is a critical mistake.

All disruptive reorganizing activities have an impact on people. A change does not need to be a full-fledged reorganization to be disruptive, even devastating, to the people involved. It is imperative that leaders consider any change that impacts the way people work and interact to be an important structural change that has great significance for their business. Organizations suffer because of ill-advised change implementation. The changes may be brilliant but poorly administered.

We will examine the process starting with a germ of an idea and carrying it through the execution phases to identify leverage points that have a profound impact on outcomes. In reality, the business world presents a continuous parade of improvement opportunities for any organization. The function of leaders is to decide which ones to develop and execute.

Trust and culture are recurring themes, because they are the most important ingredients in unlocking the potential for organizational integrations. This book delivers insight on how to build and maintain trust, even when draconian or challenging actions are being contemplated.

Trust in Transition will:

- Present a two-sided model contrasting the mechanical side of a change process with the cultural side of the same change effort.
- Explain the role that trust plays in creating successful change and teach you how to create and maintain it.
- Explore how leaders can make far more effective structural changes in order to improve the trajectory of their business.
- Give a clear view of the pitfalls and what to avoid. Learn the steps to take as well as the symptoms to watch out for.
- Explore problems in execution that increase the risk of failure.
- Discuss specific antidotes for each issue presented and the actions that will make reorganization efforts more effective.
- Walk through a recovery process to help impacted people recover equilibrium.

These concepts are easily applicable to every organization. This book boils the issues down to the smallest denominator—human interaction. As long as people are involved, these concepts and techniques will apply and enhance your ability to merge two different groups into a single functioning unit. Conceptualizing how to put two completely different groups together can lead to successful creative solutions.

While this work identifies the various problems and their root causes, the emphasis is on tools, techniques, and the positive steps that can be taken throughout integration to ensure a better result for all stakeholders. It is critical to design solutions to balance the benefits so that all stakeholder needs are considered, rather than to create a solution that benefits one group of stakeholders at the expense of another.

To help guide your change journey, this book offers the following additional tools:

- Key points that can improve the process are called out in each chapter along with questions and concepts to ponder.

- Video summaries of key points provide an alternative way to explore and share the information. These video segments can be found online at www.astd.org/trustintransition.

- Worksheets and checklists are presented in the text to help guide change efforts, or open some helpful dialogue on important topics to address.

- Diagnostic evaluations to test your organization's readiness to perform a change activity are provided. This precursor is a great way to reduce the probability of problems when the real action gets started. Each evaluation can be customized to fit your specific situation by editing or expanding on the questions provided.

Why We Make Changes

Most change occurs because the status quo is inadequate. It may be an extreme case where the business cannot pay its bills or it could be many lesser symptoms that signal an organization's inability to meet its goals or obligations. Continuing on the current path is not an option, so the leaders begin to plan a change in direction.

Change can also occur because of an opportunity to improve the future outlook. Survival under the status quo is not in question, but there is a significant opportunity to improve the future for all stakeholders. This realization prods leaders to form change strategies to capture the opportunity.

Another cause of change comes from external factors. These can be in the political, technological, geospatial, or legal environments in which the organization operates or the market in which the organization sells its goods or services. Success in a global workplace requires flexible organizations that adapt well to change.

Regardless of the impetus, once the need for change is recognized, it is followed by a strategic and tactical decision process to identify which option will produce the best result. This planning phase is a prime opportunity for leaders to set the course for the organization's future. If the decisions are wise and well executed, the organization will thrive. If the path is flawed or implemented poorly, the organization is at risk.

Choose the Right Change

Change initiatives can take hundreds of different forms based on the paths leaders select. Here are just a few examples for clarity:

- incorporating a new philosophy like "Lean" manufacturing
- reorganizing for better market penetration
- developing new technology to enable a better product
- improving employee engagement through an organization development initiative
- changing the business structure.

There are two main challenges here. The first is how to decide what makes sense. With thousands of opportunities, leaders need wisdom and patience to not become enamored with a solution too early. The analysis phase needs to be objective and applied fairly for all relevant possibilities, including changes done in several phases. Next leaders must share the benefits in a way that gets people excited about the idea. A brilliant vision can fail if it is rejected by the people who define the culture.

Understand the Risks

Would you get on an airplane if you knew the chances of having a problem, even a crash, were more than 70 percent? Of course not!

Then why are so many CEOs anxious to get involved with reorganizations in an effort to make improvements? Most reorganization efforts produce disappointing results. Estimates of failure rates for mergers, acquisitions, and other reorganizing initiatives run from 50 percent to 80 percent, depending on the author and the criteria used to define "success." If success means living up to the performance expectations of the change effort within three years, the failure rate is at the higher end of the range: 80 percent (Selden and Colvin, 2003).

Given the financial risks involved in change efforts, it is important to find ways to improve the odds. This book presents a new framework and approach with solutions to perpetual problems in the change process.

Understanding the Causes of Failure

The prime cause of failure is a form of self-deception by leaders. When contemplating reorganization, most benefits are tangible and can be estimated rather easily. If an organization merges with another company, their market share may increase. There may be new products to sell. These benefits are tangible and visible, but they may be overstated.

On the cost side, things are not as precise. Costs can be reduced by cutting redundant staff, but failures in cultural integration can increase costs in ways that are hard to predict. We know that integration is going to take time and cost money to accomplish. We can make some vague estimates of how long it will take to merge the cultures. We can try to figure out how much additional training is required. The problem is that the things that impact these intangible costs are more hidden than the hard financial benefits, so the true cost of cultural integration is hard to predict.

Often, top leaders have an unbalanced view of the cost-benefit ratio and become over-sold on the venture from the start, seeing benefits that are real and tantalizing. Sure, there are going to be costs and problems, they say, but "we can work through them." This assumption is a formula for poor results.

When leaders fall in love with the idea of the reorganization, it leaves them more likely to closed minded about the dangers. A mindset emerges from the fog of "the deal" where the top leaders are "going for it," and if people bring up legitimate questions or concerns, they are labeled "not team players" and sent packing. Once word gets out about the punishment for people who speak up, nobody will speak up about problems or issues, which creates a runaway train on the track at full throttle. This dynamic is one root cause for the poor track record for reorganizations.

Take Preventive Steps to Avoid the Traps

There are three potential antidotes that can save your organization from making a costly error in a reorganization. First, during the planning phase, there will be numerous estimates of the return-on-investment (ROI) for the project. The return calculation relies on estimates of benefits and costs. An easy solution is to allow the benefits estimates to stand, but inflate the costs using some multiplier applied to the original estimates. For example, multiply the time to complete the integration by a factor of three (you apply your own estimate). Multiply the impact of loss of customer goodwill by about five, then run the ROI calculation again to see if the change initiative is still a good business decision. If not, it would be wise to do some more research upfront on the real costs of the integration or to find a way to mitigate these costs with a proper investigation into the cultural and human implications of major changes.

A second antidote is to anoint a devil's advocate. It is critical to have someone on the senior team who can challenge assumptions without being clobbered for it. The devil's advocate must be someone in a senior position, but not the prime driver of the effort (the leader who is head over heels in love with the concept). She has to be someone the senior managers respect enough to actually listen to and consider her points. Often the devil's advocate slows down the process or causes great unrest within the senior team, so it needs to be made clear to everyone that this person has been appointed as the official PITA (pain in the "rear") on this reorganization project. It takes a special person to operate effectively as the devil's advocate, but this role can be extremely important to provide ballast for otherwise overzealous executives.

The third solution is to make the issue of cultural integration part of the decision-making process before deciding on any reorganization and then make it part of the planning all the way through the change process.

Taking these three preventive steps will not guarantee a smooth reorganization process, but it will reduce the probability of going into the process partially blind.

Once the decision to proceed with some kind of change effort has been made, the focus must turn to ensuring that the goals are reached. The solutions in the remainder of this book are intended to combat the most common problems that occur during integration. By understanding these techniques, you will increase your company's chance for success.

Food for Thought

1. Think about a reorganization you have been through that did not work out well and try to identify the root cause of the failure. Was there a way to save the effort?

2. List the qualifications for a good devil's advocate.

3. Name some of the danger signs in everyday conversation that would alert you that top executives are overzealous about a change effort.

4. Try to identify a change initiative that would make a major improvement in your current organization. Think about why you made this particular selection. Would others in your organization agree with you?

Part II:

Change Models

In this section we will look at two models of performing organizational transitions, using a merger as an example. In one model, we look at some of the symptoms that create problems or barriers. The second view looks at solutions.

1

The Classic Barrier Model

~~~~~~

"Life is what happens to you while you're busy making other plans."

John Lennon

In this chapter you will learn:

- There are two change processes that go on in parallel. One side deals with the mechanical parts of the reorganization process, and the other side concerns how the change impacts people and the whole corporate culture.

- The level of trust at the start determines the success of any reorganization.

- Reorganization efforts fail when cultures don't merge successfully.

Let's put a major change process as it typically happens under a microscope to see what is going on beneath the surface. From that examination there will be tangible recommendations that can make a huge improvement in the success of a change initiative. We will use a merger as an example.

Two Processes

What may look like a single process from the outside is really two processes going on simultaneously. While many leaders focus on the mechanical aspects of the merger, their actions are being noticed and processed through the corporate cultures, often sending shockwaves through both organizations.

Figure 1.1 is a representation of the dual processes. On the left side is a flow chart of the Mechanical Process where the valuations are determined and the financial deal is created. The right side of the chart is the Cultural Process that is going on simultaneously. The Cultural Process contains the responses of people who are caught in the tidal wave of events they cannot control.

The actions are in the larger shapes and the people involved are in the rectangular boxes off to the side. In the middle is a list of the barriers that are diminishing trust during the process.

The classic approach to reorganizations fosters an "us versus them" mentality that puts walls between the leaders in the know and the rest of the employees who can only speculate. These walls erode the trust that is so necessary for business success. They make it more difficult for the managers to do their important work and infinitely more difficult for the people in the organization to have trust in their management, both during the process and afterward.

Figure 1.1: The Classic Barrier Model

Mechanical Process		Barriers	Cultural Process	
People Involved	Activity	Type of Wall	Situation	People
Senior leaders	Developing ideas	Low trust	Performing in a steady state	Both organizations
Advisors	Performing initial research	Visits by strangers	Starting early rumors	Employee cliques
Bankers	Engaging in early discussions	Leaders gone a lot	Growing fears	Human resources
Other party	Conducting due diligence	Off-limits rooms	Loss of morale	Union officials
Accountants	Negotiating the deal	Playing games or lack of honesty	Performing damage control	Suppliers and vendors
Managers	Announcing the merger	Confusion	Dealing with fear and panic	All staff
Senior team	Deciding who leaves	Incomplete information	Holding it together	Head hunters
Entire staff	Finishing the integration	Low trust	Managing the transition	Employees

Developing the Idea/Steady State

Any merger starts out as a gleam in the eye of a senior leader, often the CEO. Some leaders just get restless if things have remained the same for a few years. They think there must be a better existence out there somewhere, so they begin to look. The impetus may be defensive (a financial crisis) or offensive (a potential expansion), but the result is the same.

Next there is a small and very quiet investigation of some ideas to find a reason or perhaps a combination of reasons to proceed.

Before long, the idea has become more tangible and the focus narrows on one type of solution: a merger. Typically, a merger follows a process that will receive most of the attention from this point on because the vast majority of mergers are a "you bet your company" type of decision.

The Cultural Process starts in the steady state configuration, where people were unaware of any discontinuity because there was none. As soon as the CEO decides that a merger may be helpful, the chemistry starts to change. If the prior behaviors of leaders have created fear or at least uncertainty about the future, then people will be edgy about what secret plans may be coming. This history of low trust will cause problems as the process continues.

Performing Initial Research/Early Rumors

The Mechanical Process gets all of management's attention, as they do the initial research and bring in experts to discuss possible moves. The idea is still developing at this point and subject to changes that will impact the success of the venture.

Perhaps nobody is saying anything about a merger, but it is clear something different is going on. Attempts to hide the discussions make for an interesting charade. It is illegal to divulge information that will materially impact the company valuation until a deal is struck, so for several months there is an uneasy atmosphere where people know something is happening, but there is no official confirmation of it.

It is impossible to hide the hundreds of signals that go on every day with special closed-door meetings, strange lawyers wandering around, people whispering to each other, and the body language of nervous executives. Nobody is fooled; they are just don't know the true impact and details. That kind of backdrop is most concerning because it lowers trust. People playing games and telling half-truths takes a toll on trust, and there is no completely adequate solution. The real barrier here is the presence of different people and no explanation of what they are doing. Without any communication, management appears to be insensitive to how people might be interpreting these activities.

Engaging in Early Discussions/Growing Fears

Often with the hiring of outside help, the official process steps begin. It is critical to recognize that a parallel process has also started, which the CEO did not intend, but has happened anyway. Word has gotten out that some interesting discussions are occurring in the corner office, and people in the organization are whispering about what might be happening.

The leaders are much less visible than before. They go to meetings off-site, and when they are in the building, they are having heavy discussions. When employees are most in need of information, the leaders are inaccessible, and that creates a barrier that further lowers trust.

Regardless of information flow, there are bound to be growing fears about the future and those fears create rumors. The most difficult part about these rumors is that they take on a life of their own and often picture a future that is bleaker than reality. When there is a void of credible information, people fill in the situation with information of their own (often untrue) invention.

Conducting Due Diligence/Morale Loss

Due diligence is where each party is allowed access to all relevant information about the other party. The objective is to disclose all information in a confidential way so there are no surprises, and the negotiation can be based on facts. The due diligence process can be short or long depending on the desires of each party, the complexity of the deal, and the trust level between the entities.

In *The Speed of Trust*, Stephen M.R. Covey tells the story of how Warren Buffet of Berkshire Hathaway once completed a $23 billion acquisition of McLane Distribution from Wal-Mart with a two-hour meeting and a handshake. This was possible because the two parties trusted each other going into the meeting. In an interview for the book Buffet said: "We did no 'due diligence.' We knew everything would be as Wal-Mart said it would be—and it was."

The due diligence phase is a good place to test the integrity of each party. You should not play games. The idea is to disclose whatever the other party wants to know honestly, in order to avoid surprises later. Of course, this is extremely difficult to manage with 100 percent transparency.

The attention to the detail, plus all the cleanup work in preparation for due diligence, does not go unnoticed by people in the organization. The whole parade of cleaning and inspection steps cannot be hidden from view, so the rumor mill begins to make their own explanations.

A data room often is created for convenience. Access to the room is carefully controlled to include only those executives who need to know. Usually, the room is locked and the windows are covered so that people cannot see what happens inside. Having a secret room where data is being analyzed creates a wall that demoralizes people in the organization. It is further evidence that something big is happening, but the employees are not allowed to know what it is.

Negotiations/Damage Control

The negotiation process has been going on for months at this point, but the legal meeting to determine the financial deal has not happened yet. Negotiations are commonly done off-site because it is more convenient to negotiate without any interruptions. Hotel conference rooms are often used for negotiating sessions because the visiting team can stay at the hotel. It becomes a kind of bunker where both teams live to work toward an agreement. Another format has the parties meet at the office of one of the lawyers involved in the deal. The location of the negotiation has a lot to do with the outcome because it influences the power of each party.

The wall here is that the leaders are operating a secret deal that comes off as a mystery to the rest of the company. There may be times when the discussions break down and cause anxiety for executives. The struggle for employees is in trying to interpret the abnormal actions and demeanor of their leaders.

Once employees are aware of and upset by the secret change, it is time for damage control. This means paying attention to the emotional decline, even if you cannot make people feel great about what is going on at the moment. Good communication is essential. Managers at all levels need to listen to the rumor mill and answer questions as best they can even if they cannot share everything that is happening.

Do not deceive people. First of all, it does not work. People have an amazing aptitude for picking up smoke screens. They can tell as much by the body language of the leaders as by what they say. In fact, if there is a discrepancy between the body language and the words being used, employees will believe the body language nearly every time.

Announcing the Merger/Uncertainty and Panic

Once the company makes the deal, it is time to roll out the news. In some cases, organizations do a careful job of informing the employees first and explaining the significance. Other times, the employees hear the dreaded news through the media. Someone's wife will call him up at work and say, "I just heard on the news that your company has been sold." You would think that kind of callous indifference to employees would never happen, but it happens every day. The same holds true for announcements of lesser significance.

When the announcement is made all employees realize they will be affected in some way. The shockwave going through the organization resembles an earthquake. At this point, many managers make a huge mistake. They tend to hide in their offices or go into briefing meetings so they are unavailable to their shocked workers. This practice tends to amplify the damage. Once the merger is announced people generally go into a kind of shock. They can still function, but they have lost their bearings. For one thing, they are not sure they will have a job, and even if they do, they are not sure what will change. If leaders do not have enough information on what will be happening, the incomplete story does little to assuage their employees' panic.

Along with shock comes a bit of relief that the news is finally out. Often the reality is not nearly as bad as the persistent rumors made it out to be. For example, the rumor might have been that the entire operation was going to be outsourced and the plant closed. The reality may be that the operation has been sold to a strong organization that really needs the expertise and processes of the existing operation, so in fact, the future may be brighter than before and a whole lot better than anticipated.

Deciding Who Leaves

Deciding who leaves and who stays takes on many different forms. Typically the managers decide how large the merged staff should be and then they do a ranking of resources. This usually takes some time, so there is great angst and loss of focus among the workforce—another barrier to trust. People continue to work during the transition, but productivity is compromised. The needs of the customers receive less attention as people are worried about their own survival. People just do the best they can, try to cope with the uncertainty, and eagerly wait for more information from management.

I have coached numerous people and groups through this part of the process, and the best word to describe how they feel is "powerless." They care about what is happening, but recognize they have very little say in it. They worry, but try to keep their heads down so they do not get chopped off. Managers deal with the uncertainty for themselves while trying to project a calm attitude to the people below. For example, "you should feel good that you have a job." For the employees, hearing those words does not elicit comfort; they bring out justifiable rage. If this stage lasts for any significant time, the business will suffer irrevocable damage.

Completing the Integration

With the mechanical steps completed, leaders begin to put the pieces back together and determine the processes that will govern the merged organization. Slowly, some framework starts to emerge, and people begin to accept their fate and make contributions to the new company. It is in making a contribution that the healing begins. The whole process is grueling for individuals and their families who only want stability and security.

At this point, any trust in the combined organization and leaders is in shambles, which is a huge barrier on the road to success. Compounding the loss of internal trust, the employees are now in a position where they must try to trust their counterparts in the other part of the organization. They often know very little about the other culture and are skeptical at every signal that comes along. The end result is that the merger is off to a very shaky start. It is no wonder that the success rate for mergers and acquisitions (M&As) is so low.

While the personal angst plays out, the combined organization is not focusing on the basics of business. The supply chain is changing, so the flow of product will be compromised. The sales organization is not capable of telling customers what is going on, so there is a noticeable dip in sales. Customer service is confused because the lineup of products is now different. Billing and other administrative functions are changing. Both sides of the new business are in disarray as people focus their energies elsewhere. Just trying to get the product out the door and not lose customers is incredibly difficult at the start of an integration.

Cautionary Tales

Let's look at examples of unsuccessful mergers that illustrate what can happen if the cultural aspects are not considered to the extent they should be.

Daimler-Chrysler Merger

The 1998 merger of Daimler-Benz of Stuttgart, Germany, and Chrysler Corporation of Detroit, Michigan, was billed as a merger of equals. The product lines were similar but did not totally overlap, so the market position was favorable for both organizations. Investors never really believed that it was a merger of equals and suggested it was really Daimler taking over the weakened Chrysler. The principle idea for the merger was synergies in manufacturing and marketing while allowing two iconic brands to coexist in the marketplace. Chrysler had been the perennial third place automobile company in the United States behind General Motors and Ford.

The deal did not work out as planned. Daimler sold the unit to Cerberus Capital Management in 2007 for $6 billion after a series of financial setbacks for Chrysler after the merger. The reason for the break up was that the culture of Chrysler never integrated with Daimler's formal organization and very rigid culture. Daimler's management style was formal in reporting structure and even dress code. Chrysler was much less formal, with a cowboy management style and informal dress code. From the start, the Daimler rules were impressed upon the American company, and the difference in style took a toll every day. Even conference calls and email exchanges were stressful.

Originally billed as a merger of equals, it became a takeover situation that lasted 10 contentious years. The monetary loss to Daimler ultimately reached more than $36 billion. That number is hard to fathom, so think of it as a $10 million loss every day for a decade.

The basic problem was simply the inability of the two different cultures to get along. Had the organizational cultures been studied in advance and the leadership work been done to blend the cultures or leave them autonomous, the tribulations could have been prevented.

P&G's Acquisition of Gillette

Getting cultures to mesh is a giant task worthy of a master strategist. It is often the little differences between the groups that can irritate people enough to become large obstacles for integration.

It is rather like a marriage where the couple is obviously in love. They have a great deal of respect and shared goals and values—but they still find areas of friction in the little things, like the toothpaste tube cap or the toilet seat position. It is often not the macroscopic ideological alignment that causes marriages to fail, but the little daily annoyances. This is something to keep in mind when trying to get corporate cultures to mesh.

A case in point is the acquisition of Gillette by Proctor & Gamble (P&G) in 2005. These two titans of consumer products were well aligned in terms of product strategies and marketing. The integration should have been easy, right? Wrong! Just ask CEO A.G. Lafley who tried for years to get the cultures to work well together. It was the little style differences that kept getting in the way. For example, Gillette was used to driving fast decisions by getting consensus using online memos, while P&G took a more methodological approach using face-to-face meetings to drive decisions. Ray Fisman (2013) wrote an article in *Slate* magazine entitled "Culture Clash" about the struggle to merge the two cultures. He wrote, "You'd think these sorts of cultural hurdles would be easy to overcome, especially given the promise of strong technological and strategic advantages. Yet attempts to get disparate groups to work with one another—whether across departments or across companies—are often fraught with unanticipated complications and misunderstandings."

It took several years and a considerable investment to make progress in the P&G/Gillette integration. They made progress by employing a special cultural integration task force to help individuals and groups concentrate on areas of agreement and become more tolerant of style idiosyncrasies.

Summary

We have worked through the model and looked at examples of failed mergers in a condensed view of the main steps. It is important to understand that the actual process may contain hundreds of steps, numerous meetings, thousands of financial calculations, months of negotiation, and a lot of distraction from business as usual.

With the corporate culture falling deeper into a trust deficit while leaders are focused on the mechanical process to actually cut a deal and reconfigure the business, it is a huge challenge not to slip backward on all levels. These barriers to trust can be turned into bridges that enable the organization to withstand trauma and uncertainty with grace and perhaps even maintain trust during this difficult period. Leaders must learn to consider trust levels and corporate cultures in the planning and execution of the change initiative.

Food for Thought

1. Looking at the two-sided flow chart of the process, think back to a reorganization you were a part of and identify which areas were done well and which ones went badly.

2. Assess the level of trust in your current organization. What steps could be done immediately to encourage trust?

2

A Better Way

"If you run into a wall, don't turn around and give up. Figure out how to climb it, go through it, or work around it."

Michael Jordan

In this chapter you will learn:

- There are walls between the two sides of the process.
- Those walls can be made into bridges with some effort.

The Importance of Trust

The success of the entire change process depends on trust—the trust level before integration and the trust maintained during the process. With the Barrier Model, the trust level usually starts low and gets lower throughout the process, contributing to the high failure rate of change initiatives. Let's break the trust issue down into finer detail to reveal some interesting dynamics to build a better model.

Obviously, the best situation is where there is high trust in both organizations before the turmoil begins. People believe in their leaders and have faith that the actions taken in the past have been a balance of what is good for the business and what is good for the employees. The workforce feels supported and appreciated. A kind of family atmosphere and goodwill exists at most levels. Sure there are some disgruntled people sprinkled about both groups, but the general atmosphere is positive and upbeat.

With this precursor, the proposed merger can proceed pretty well. People will be tolerant of the lack of specific information, at least for a while, because they have faith in their leaders. The trust level will provide a prophylactic effect as some of the deliberations happen. Because both groups have a positive, trusting environment, the leaders involved can focus on the negotiation and not be distracted with keeping people calm while simultaneously trying to get the best possible deal. This environment allows for a much faster negotiation process, which benefits everyone in both organizations.

Trust is built with a lot of honest communication, and that pattern must be continued throughout the period of uncertainty. Legal restrictions provide a significant challenge for communication, but they should not be used as a reason to go silent. The flow of information may be restricted, but it should not stop. Telling people the truth, that "there are things we cannot divulge for legal reasons," will be accepted in a high trust environment. Another approach is to simply indicate that this is a trust based organization, and people will need to have faith that decisions will be made in the best interest of everyone, long term. Either way, people will draw conclusions that cannot be confirmed or denied for legal reasons.

The other extreme is the worst condition. If neither group is going in with any kind of trust between the workers and the leaders, the entire process will be difficult. Without trust there is no basis for people to believe any information provided by the leader, so instead they will believe what they want.

The lack of trust on both sides is at least partially due to the abusive behaviors of leaders in the past, and that is not going to change if they seclude themselves for negotiation. Therefore, the situation deteriorates quickly during the dealings, and sabotage, strikes, or other extreme forms of rebellion are common. Of course, having buildings on fire, figuratively or literally, is not going to be helpful to the negotiating process. There is little hope for a viable business entity to emerge on the other side.

In between those extremes, you have a very interesting condition where one group has higher trust than the other. When you think about it, that is always the condition to some degree. In this case, the team where trust is low will be at a significant disadvantage in the negotiation.

Groups with low trust have more things that they need to hide in the due diligence process. They have lower energy because they are fighting on two fronts. They have less reliable information coming out of their own organization. They cannot rely on their people to rally behind the cause of a successful integration. The leaders have less skill in general, which puts them at greater risk during the negotiation.

Also important is the power balance between the two organizations. The group holding more cards has an advantage they can play during the negotiation. The dynamic interaction of power and trust creates an infinite variety of conditions that are situational. It is important to have a good baseline of trust and power going into a negotiation because it impacts how the discussions will go. In every change effort, the team that has higher trust going in will have a significant advantage throughout the process. They will be the stronger team and normally get the best results because they can focus on the negotiation with fewer distractions.

After the announcement, managers will ask people to work together in the integration process. They will say "Sure, some people will have to leave, but be a good sport and work diligently for the cause." That is not going to happen in a low trust environment.

If trust in one company is lacking going into a reconfiguration, trust in the other company will usually be even lower. If we do not trust our own leaders, it is unlikely we are going to trust the leaders of the "enemy." It becomes a situation where the basis for doing business at all must be rebuilt from the ground up.

A positive result is much more likely if both organizations have reasonable trust to begin with. People will listen to the combined leadership voice and give it a chance. They will be skeptical of the leaders they do not know, but there will be a quiet confidence that these must be good people if their leaders chose to work with them.

At lower levels, the workforce is likely to picture a group of capable people, just like themselves. They realize that there have to be cuts, but they believe the best people will remain for the future.

The Bridge Model

By understanding the advantages of trust and focusing on corporate culture in times of change, we can build better processes to lead and manage change. By using the Bridge Model, management has an opportunity to manage the transition to keep trust at its highest possible level. We now have the opportunity to turn walls into bridges that can facilitate progress. Following these ideas well can lead to a better result from reorganization. Let's look at the diagram with bridges replacing the walls.

Figure 2.1: The Bridge Model

Mechanical Process		Bridges	Cultural Process	
People Involved	Activity		Situation	People
Senior leaders	Developing ideas	History of trust	Performing in a steady state	Both organizations
Advisors	Performing initial research	Sharing the strategy	Starting early rumors	Employee cliques
Bankers	Engaging in early discussions	Communicate	Growing fears	Human resources
Other party	Conducting due diligence	Involve people	Loss of morale	Union officials
Accountants	Negotiating the deal	Neutral territory	Performing damage control	Suppliers and vendors
Managers	Announcing the merger	Greater communication	Dealing with fear and panic	All staff
Senior team	Deciding who leaves	Timely actions	Holding it together	Head hunters
Entire staff	Finishing the integration	Good measures	Managing the transition	Employees

In this model, the left side is identical to the Barrier Model, but now we have worked to construct bridges so that the process on the right side is more manageable and optimistic. There is more communication and interaction across the bridges, so the outcome is vastly different.

Developing Ideas/Steady State

If you have built an environment of high trust, the whole process will be easier. In this culture the steady state organization in both groups is working reasonably well and people feel valued. They expect that their leaders will have ideas—some that are shared and some that will be shared at a later date. They are willing to listen and to consider how they may be impacted with more objectivity and less fear. Whatever level of trust exists at the start, they recognize that maintaining it and growing it, even in uncertain times, is the best way to make the merger successful.

Performing Initial Research/Rumors

During initial data gathering, the bridge is for leaders to share that they are looking for strategic ways to strengthen the business. People need to be told proactively that something is going on rather than trying to figure it out by observing leaders. Sharing the broad strategy can be done without revealing data that is inappropriate. This strategy makes people feel more comfortable, so trust is not immediately swamped by rumors.

Engaging in Early Discussions

Even though early discussions must be kept under tight control for legal reasons, leaders can still communicate the intent to strengthen the business. If employees are treated like adults who are able to deal with the change, trust will be maintained, even without complete disclosure. With a track record of good communication, people will be patient with leaders who cannot share everything at the start of the process. They will understand the need for some processes that are not entirely visible.

Conducting Due Diligence

The due diligence process can occur with participation from a wider group of employees. They do not need to know who the other party is (or even that there is another party) to be able to share information about their own department. As the data room becomes populated, it is wise provide some information to more people. This expands awareness, so there needs to be control, but that is possible in a high trust organization. In a high trust organization, people will keep information confidential if told to do so, which means that lower level people can become part of the process. It really helps build trust when people other than the top executives are included in the action.

Obviously you cannot involve the entire workforce, but you can have key people engaged in the process by asking them to help gather data, participate in due diligence, brainstorm options, identify hurdles, list strategies, and even rank people. The key to involvement is to be creative rather than secretive.

You do not need to divulge details of the deal in order to involve employees in the process. For example, a group leader can assemble training records of employees, an HR generalist can record union nego-tiations, a supervisor can extract production or attendance records, or a quality manager can summarize ISO 9000 compliance records.

Negotiating the Deal/Commitment

One key is to handle negotiations in neutral territory so that specific information can be closely guarded. Having a neutral territory creates a bridge that allows both entities to include more people in the data anal-ysis phase without compromising legal requirements.

If the meetings are held primarily in the home offices of one participant, that group has a large advantage. You may find yourself working around issues of territory and missing some important points in due diligence. The better approach is to take over a hotel somewhere and use their boardroom or other well-appointed conference area for the deliberations. The only caution here is to be sure the room has the necessary equipment for the level of work to be done. Do not select a room without the facilities to capture agreements efficiently and display data.

As more people have been involved in the data gathering and options process, they will be much more committed to the entire process and have more trust that the confidential negotiations are being done to build the best future for everyone.

Announcing the Merger

When the merger is announced, it is the time to increase communication, not become more secretive. The legal restriction is now lifted, so there is no barrier to full disclosure. By the time the merger is announced, the top leaders are often tired and forget that the work of merging cultures is just starting. Successful integration relies on excellent communication.

It is important to get a summary communication out as quickly as possible. If this is a large merger the press is going to be all over it, so have a well-crafted statement go out to employees as soon as possible. Then start meeting with groups of people to give details and answer questions as frankly as possible.

One thing to avoid saying is, "We are going to merge with ABC Company. We have not yet figured out all the details of what jobs will be cut, so just hang in there and we will let you know as soon as we can." Instead, say, "It is up to all of us to create a successful high trust organization as we integrate the two groups. We intend to have maximum involvement of everyone during that process, so we can capture the best ideas from all of you and create a new future together. It will take some time to sort out, but we will do this together and with high integrity."

Deciding Who Leaves

There are two schools of thought on the process of cutting staff. Some advocate cutting deep and fast, and there is a case to be made for that strategy. If you decide on general staffing levels and get the layoff announcements out quickly, you can clear the air so that people begin to relax. A long period of uncertainty will allow some of the most valuable employees to seek employment elsewhere.

The alternate approach is to do a first round of layoffs where obvious overlap is evident and there is an easy choice between those who need to stay and those who should go. Then, you can allow the rest of the reconfiguring to play out more slowly with the involvement of the team. The upside of this is that with more involvement, there will be higher commitment and tolerance for a period of uncertainty. My observation is that when people have a real say in how the jobs are configured, they buy in to the staffing levels much better.

The dynamics of the companies involved and the situation will determine which approach to take. It is a judgment call which philosophy to use, but it is important to make that call consciously and not by default.

It is not good to stretch out the process too long. Some organizations try to lengthen the process, thinking that it means less pain in the end. Think of it as removing a bandage from a skinned knee. You can remove the bandage very slowly and experience pain for a long time, or you can rip it off quickly and experience the same pain but for a shorter duration.

In this regard, it is well to heed the advice of John Wooden, the famous basketball coach. He said, "You must be quick, but never hurry." Take the time required to do things right, but do not drag things out—let the process determine the pace.

Listen carefully to people as they describe how much work can be accomplished by a single person. Do not cut so much that you set people up for failure; make sure there are enough resources so you have time to build the integrated culture. Many organizations make the mistake of cutting so many people in the initial announcement that everyone ends up in a state of overload and no organizational development work is possible, which means the organization is not likely to mesh very well.

Completing the Integration

The process of successful integration is the most important part of a merger. By this time, the deal has been struck and at least the initial downsizing has been completed. It is time to rebuild the organization as one entity. Some organizations elect to continue operations as two groups as if no merger had transpired and slowly move toward a merged state. This is a dangerous strategy because polarization will become more pronounced in the future. Instead, create a vision of a fully integrated culture and start blending the organization by making smart moves with key people.

It is best to start a new strategic process with the combined team where you develop vision, mission, values, and behaviors statements. Then do a SWOT analysis to take stock of assets and conditions. Finally, distill a unified strategy (not two strategies) along with tactics and action items. There should be high involvement from both camps. One of the key strategies must be to generate a unified organization with high trust.

A good framework starts the progress, but you need to continually measure progress to shore up areas where there are issues. Metrics are what drive the organization forward. Good metrics create good behaviors, whereas poorly designed metrics create actions opposed to the vision. To be helpful, metrics need to drive the right behaviors. That sounds simple enough, yet there are numerous situations where metrics lead an organization in exactly the wrong direction. For example, an organization wanted to increase revenue for their high end disk drives. The CEO studied the data and noticed that the salesmen who made the most sales calls were the top revenue generators. He put a measure in place that rewarded each person on the salesforce based on how many calls he or she made in a month.

The results of the new policy were amazing. Revenue decreased by over 30 percent. By rewarding each salesperson on the number of calls, each person generated a lot more calls and did not worry much about closing the sale at end of the calls. What seemed like a positive measure actually drove negative results.

Another example occurred when an industrial firm wanted to improve employee satisfaction based on their annual survey. The HR manager noted that personnel development showed a direct correlation to employee satisfaction and retention. He established a metric that would track the number of training hours per employee per year.

The training metric incentivized managers to train people on unnecessary skills, and forced workers to go to class, even if it meant having to stay extra time to get the work done. The employees hated the training mandate because it did not make sense. The metric showed that employees were being trained more, but the actual employee satisfaction was much lower during the next survey. The metric had actually done the opposite of what was intended because it was not well executed. The lesson here is that the metric must be good and applied well or you stand a good chance of driving the wrong behaviors.

An Example to Follow

Now that you have identified the expected behaviors, the objectives or goals, and the metrics that drive them, it is time to start rebuilding. First, review the example of the Disney-Pixar merger for some inspiration.

Disney-Pixar Merger

In contrast to the Daimler-Chrysler merger, the Disney-Pixar situation was more of an acquisition than a merger of equals, but the differing cultures were still an issue. This acquisition was ultimately successful, although most people would not have predicted that at the outset. Let's examine why.

It was a David and Goliath situation from the start. Pixar was formed in 1987 shortly after Steve Jobs left Apple. It was a high-end computer processing organization that made image-converting equipment. After a rocky start, Pixar eventually focused on computer animation software and provided content for many Disney films. According to the *New York Times*, Pixar made a $26 million deal with Disney to produce three computer-animated feature films, the first of which was *Toy Story*.

Toy Story created a lot of stress between Pixar and Disney. It was the mid-1990s, and Jobs, who was the CEO of Pixar at the time, had a lot of personal animosity for Michael Eisner, then CEO of Disney. The two organizations operated with completely different styles. Pixar had an entrepreneurial and informal style, while Disney was a bureaucratic behemoth. Mostly they fought over the revenue split from successful films. Pixar was responsible for the creation and production, while Disney handled promotion and distribution. Profits and production costs were split 50-50, but Disney exclusively owned all story and sequel rights and also collected a distribution fee. The lack of rights was perhaps the most onerous aspect to Pixar and set the stage for a contentious relationship.

Jobs despised Eisner so much that there were no serious discussions about merging until after Eisner left Disney in 2005. Bob Iger, who had a very different approach to the issues involving Pixar, replaced Eisner as CEO of Disney. The relationship thawed enough that Disney acquired Pixar in 2006. The move gave Jobs the largest share of Disney stock, so he joined the board of directors at Disney. Iger decided not to try to dictate the culture at Pixar or make it conform to the culture at Disney. That was a very wise move. In fact, they went so far as to create a tangible list of the things that Pixar did not need to change. Iger had learned some painful lessons earlier when he dealt with integration at his former company, ABC, so he decided to modify his style at Disney. Allowing Pixar the freedom to maintain their culture made the acquisition highly successful. Again we see that it is the culture rather than the assets that becomes a major hurdle, or enabler, of a consolidation effort. In this case, because the top leader allowed the cultures to operate separately, rather than force one group to drastically change its culture, a completely different result was obtained. This acquisition was successful because the two groups had unique functions, and were allowed to retain their cultural norms.

Summary

There are numerous other examples that point to culture as a very large issue whenever organizations consider joining forces. Too often CEOs of companies just assume that "things will work out." That attitude is a huge mistake. If things are a great fit in terms of culture, then fine. If the cultures clash, recognize there is a long, hard road ahead, and maybe a crash at the end of that road.

Going through the merger process in a way that encourages rather than destroys trust allows the integrated unit a chance at success. Working through a solid and efficient strategic process allows the company to focus on those key things that will foster the best performance. Holding people accountable for the metrics in the right way will make it happen in a way that enhances trust.

Food for Thought

1. If there is low trust in the other side of the entity, what steps can be taken to improve the relationship?

2. Name several ways that people in the organization can participate more in the process without violating confidentiality.

3

Consider All Stakeholders

"Find the appropriate balance of competing claims by various groups of stakeholders. All claims deserve consideration but some claims are more important than others."

Warren G. Bennis

In this chapter you will learn:

- Decisions on reorganization must satisfy a balance of the stakeholders of the business, not just the owners.
- The six categories of stakeholders are: shareholders, employees, customers, suppliers and logistics partners, communities, and the environment.

The holistic approach described in this chapter adds depth to the merger models. It is important to set objectives and view them from the vantage point of each of the important stakeholder groups before working on specific solutions to potential problems. In each case, these objectives must include steps toward higher trust that create pathways to stakeholder satisfaction.

Shareholders

All levels of supervision need management to see the benefit of the move in the long run. The shareholders, who have a financial interest in the health of the organization, also share this vantage point.

Before integration, there are two independent sets of owners. There may be some people who own shares in both organizations, but that will usually be a low percentage. If the two entities are not joined in any way before integration, the fortunes of the shareholder groups are completely separate. Before the integration neither group cares about the situation of the other group, but when the prospect of joining forces becomes evident everything changes.

Now the shareholders have an interesting dilemma. On one hand, the short-term situation relates to money, as decided in the negotiation. If one organization pays too much, then the owners of that group suffer a loss, but if they pay less than market price they gain a financial advantage. During the negotiation there is a feeling of competition between the shareholder groups, but there is life after the deal and both groups will have a vested financial interest in the future. It should not be a competition at all when the long-term prospects are considered. It is more of a cooperative or synergistic relationship if the shareholders intend to remain with the merged company.

If we are discussing an acquisition, and the selling shareholders intend to take the proceeds from the sale and split from the venture, then the negotiation is more competitive. If the sellers leave as soon as the financial deal is struck, every dollar will come out of the pocket of their counterpart in the other organization, which makes the negotiation openly adversarial.

If all owners intend to remain financially tied to the merged organization, then they are not adversaries at all. They both want the same thing: the long-term success of the combined entity. They can negotiate from that stance.

Given that the managers involved in the negotiation are normally shareholders as well makes the challenge even bigger. It is important to approach the negotiation with a certain level of detachment to avoid a conflict of interest, but it is difficult not to be emotionally involved with decisions that impact one's wallet.

Employees

The second stakeholder group is the employees. Their needs are centered on stability and—hopefully—continued employment. Unfortunately the employees (often rightfully) feel like pawns in the game. Individually they have little power, but collectively they are vital for the new company.

The employees may or may not be represented by a union, and it makes a big difference if they are. In general, the existence of a collective bargaining unit to go between management and the workers makes negotiations more complex. What might be acceptable to the employees may be not approved by the union, or what the union might feel is appropriate may not feel like the best deal to the employees. Of course, there is also antagonism between the union and management. Read about some of the specific dynamics of the union situation in chapter 5.

There is usually a need to cut staff in the merged organization, and the method and timing is of high importance to this group. The expanded markets derived from a merger may potentially mean enough additional business that layoffs are minimal, but that is not often the case. The best vision for remaining employees is a stable and growing entity where they feel valued and proud to work, but since the employees feel like bystanders, their stake in the outcome often has the feeling of a life and death struggle.

For most people, their career and job are fairly high on the priority list of things to protect. The reason is simple sustenance. Getting a job in some economies is an arduous task. Often workers have the benefit of a long relationship with their current organization, so with little formal education, they have been able to work their way up into responsible and lucrative jobs based on job knowledge and dedication. Now the job is going to change, and their value in a new area may be considerably less than it is now.

These conditions explain why rumors are spread quickly and employees are intensely interested in knowing what is going to happen at all times. If there is high trust, it helps reduce much of the panic.

Customers

The third group of stakeholders is comprised of the customers of each company. Both entities have customers to serve throughout the merger period. Keeping customer delivery and service a priority is essential, or the merged organization will be severely wounded. Customers are sometimes neglected in the rush of busywork surrounding a merger, even though the customer is the reason for the change in the first place.

Before the merger was under consideration, all of the top executives in both organizations had "customer focus" at or near the top of their priority list. Now, for an extended period of time, the customer is often assumed to be a steady commodity that the lower level staff can handle while the executives are distracted. That is a false assumption. The customers from both organizations are going to feel a difference, and some of them will defect to the competition while all the negotiation is going on. The mechanical process often fails to give adequate emphasis to customer satisfaction.

Before the deal, there are two sets of customers being served by two supply chains and two customer service departments. After the deal, there is a combined set of customers being served by one supply chain and one customer service department. During the transition, all of the customers are trying to figure out what is going on, who they should call, when their next order will arrive, and countless other logistical details. Because the support structure is often in chaos with difficult office and communication integrations, the customers' needs are not always met. It only takes a couple of bad deliveries or unanswered phone calls to send valuable customers looking for an alternate supplier.

One way to ensure great customer service during the turmoil is to have a robust supply chain process. If the process to serve customer needs is so refined and well-staffed that it requires little to no management involvement, then the customer's needs are protected, at least during the negotiation process. The classic process for manufacturing organizations is the Manufacturing Resource Planning Process (MRPII).

MRPII is a system designed to help manage the supply chain, including estimates of customer needs, supplier integration, manufacturing plans, and distribution logistics. The system includes precise plans and metrics to allow the flow of products to match customer needs perfectly at all times. Building trust throughout the supply chain enables mutual synergistic relationships. These relationships create a more robust and flexible team, which is especially helpful in times of peak demand or emergency situations.

Whatever product or service is provided to the customer, it is essential to have it well documented and properly staffed to maintain excellence during the time of due diligence. Often organizations cut back on their customer service department before a merger in order to improve bottom line figures for valuation purposes. This choice is unwise because any degradation in the service level during this time will cause customer defections. Customers notice how long it takes to talk to a live person on the phone. They are also highly sensitive to changes in the patterns of service.

Once the merger is announced, the real problems hit for the customer because all of the systems and people who provide services are in turmoil. For example, the order entry staff is busy in meetings trying to figure out what the benefits package is going to be. The employees are worried about potential loss of employment. The phone systems may be in transition from the two old systems to a combined system. The ability to take orders at all may be interrupted for some time. Customers calling in will notice that things are different, but not in a good way.

The same problems will exist in the customer service department, the repairs department, the accounts receivable department, the credit department, and every single entity customers might contact to do business. All employees have to perform flawlessly if they hope to keep customers, but that is impossible when their focus is elsewhere. On and on it goes until all systems are merged and made bulletproof.

Customer defections can be devastating to any business. They represent a huge leak in the ROI calculation that was most likely not factored into the equation when the CEO originally planned the merger. There are no 100 percent solutions, but there are some precautions that can mitigate problems.

It is a mistake to prune support staff too soon and too deeply, because the ability to flex to customer demand is essential if the change is going to be transparent to the customer. Many organizations make the mistake of doing a very deep cut in service people very soon after the merger, and then they wonder why revenues show a significant dip over the next couple years. It is not hard to understand why this happens, and it is preventable.

The best way to satisfy the customer during the transition is to resolve that we must never sacrifice the customer experience in any way during the entire transition. That value needs to be imprinted in the heads of every person from the CEO to the mail clerk. If you do that and back it up with actions and decisions on a daily basis, then and only then are you protected from major loss of revenue as a result of the merger.

Suppliers and Logistics

The suppliers and logistics partners that make the organization work are the fourth group of stakeholders who need to be part of the thinking process. If vendors are consolidated, it can be done in a way that enhances rather than diminishes the resulting processes. The decisions about these external relationships will provide a backdrop of support long into the future.

When a merger occurs, you have two sets of suppliers and logistics partners. In many cases a consolidation can create opportunities for process improvements. It is also a time for making some heavy decisions that may not be popular with all partners. It can be tempting to pull the plug on vendors too early when a less expensive option is available with the higher volume. However, it is a better decision to run both for long enough to prove how robust the new configuration really is before severing ties with valuable partners. I have seen a few horror stories when the supply chain partners were cut off too early.

Community

Another important stakeholder for any organization is the local community. Decisions concerning where to place assets and offices have a large impact on the communities in which organizations reside. Heavy-handed or ill-advised closing of certain facilities can mortally wound a community. In these situations, the responsibility is a moral challenge.

To be a responsible corporate citizen, it is important to include local tax considerations, building ordinances, municipal service agreements, and employee headcounts in planning decisions. The organization needs to fit well into the community and provide its fair share of the support for community events. Communities are often willing to give tax incentives and other perks for a company to stay local, which should also be taken into consideration.

A community's location, climate, cost of living, and economic conditions make a difference to employees when it comes time to move in or out of the area, and these are things that should not be ignored when deciding where operations will be located for a combined entity.

This stakeholder may not seem as important as some of the others, and that is why it is often given less attention. Over time, an organization can get a bad reputation for neglecting community responsibilities, but it does not need to be that way. Corporations show their concern for the local community when they donate time, materials, and even money to support local causes. This is not just philanthropy: It is a sound business practice to give back to the community that supports you.

In a merger situation, there are often two communities to consider, which may even be located in different countries, so smart businesses need to establish some ground rules for their local support. It is not necessary for each unit have exactly the same support structure post-merger, but there needs to be some conscious decisions about the participation in each community.

Environment

A final stakeholder to include is the environment. In business, we make decisions every day that create various levels of environmental impact. As we consider any kind of reorganization, we must be mindful that we are custodians of a tiny slice of the world. It is not necessary to try to go out and change how other organizations or societies impact the world, but we should make the right choices about how we are affecting the planet with our decisions.

For example, in *Conscious Capitalism*, John Mackey and Raj Sisodia document a compelling case for including the environment as a key stakeholder. Mackey points to numerous initiatives at his company, Whole Foods Market. It focuses on the environment in three important areas: more sustainable livestock production, animal welfare, and seafood sustainability. In each of these areas Whole Foods has numerous initiatives that are helping the planet by feeding more people, while having a lower impact on the environment.

The authors also point to several other organizations that are doing things to help the environment and saving a lot of money at the same time. For example, Wal-Mart has major initiative to reduce product packaging and make it more recyclable, which will save $3.4 billion.

One tricky situation occurs when one part of the merged organization is located in an environmentally responsible part of the world and the other partner is located in an area known for inappropriate environmental practices. To be effective, the formal deal needs to say that both parties will operate responsibly and make green decisions going forward.

Summary

In this chapter, we reviewed six major stakeholders that must all be considered when conducting a major reorganization. No organization operates in a vacuum, and when a change in configuration is discussed, it is important to focus on the benefits to all six, rather than improving conditions for one or two of the stakeholders at the expense of the others.

In the next chapter, we will discuss the issue of size. Large corporate reorganizations or mergers get a lot of public attention, but smaller changes are just as disruptive to employees and have far greater impact on society in the aggregate.

Food for Thought

1. Some people claim that the different stakeholders have mutually exclusive goals and that you cannot satisfy one without upsetting the other. How would you rebut this notion?

2. Describe who you would include in a decision to close down a specific plant.

3. How can you explain to employees that there is a balance of objectives and not all decisions will appear to favor them?

4

The Impact of Size

"Every single time you make a merger, somebody is losing his identity. And saying something different is just rubbish."

Carlos Ghosn

In this chapter you will learn:

- Large or small reorganizations require a similar thought process, just differing rigor.
- For the people involved, the size of the action is irrelevant.
- Use a logical process and checklist to cover all the bases.

Every day in the news we hear about mega-mergers between giant organizations like airlines and automobile companies. These consolidations typically involve billions of dollars and take many months or even years to accomplish. The moves are the subject of constant Wall Street and business press analysis. They are highly regulated by the U.S. Justice Department. However, there are thousands of smaller mergers, acquisitions, or reorganizations that go on every day. Together these smaller but numerous actions dwarf the mega-mergers in terms of total impact, even though they do not get as much attention in the press.

Any activity to change the way a unit goes about accomplishing its mission is a form of change that involves reorganizing the roles of people. Unfortunately, even in smaller initiatives, the tendency is to focus on the mechanical nature of the action with little planning for integrating employees. In general, when two groups merge within a corporation, far more energy will be spent on the timing of the move and the layout of the new office than on changes that will need to be made to the way people work together during and after the merge. Putting off procedural issues until the initiative is complete misses an excellent opportunity for people to become invested in both the process and the outcome. The typical sequence almost guarantees a lapse in customer service and great anxiety among workers while managers try to sort out the mess.

The solution is to begin by addressing why a change is needed. If your company needs to find a way to be more competitive in the new world-wide market, then start by discussing this problem with the people in the organization. Take the time to solicit creative ways to solve the problem, which may or may not involve reorganization. Let those affected come to the conclusion that if the organization is to survive at all, something significant needs to be done. There is always more than one way to reach an objective and if you ask, people will have many ideas.

Involving the impacted groups will probably bring up the topic of combining units. They can help configure the setup of the merged entity and also begin to plan for the impact on individuals. They can set up groups tasked with taking care of customer issues with "one voice" while the organizational turmoil is going on. They can establish training programs for individuals who need to learn different functions. They can also help people whose jobs will be eliminated find a path to a viable future inside or outside the organization. The affected people can, and should, help figure out what to do before the transition begins.

Companies avoid involving employees because they fear impacted people might get angry and start some forms of sabotage or look for a new job. It is true that there is some risk of that kind of problem, but it is far better to take this risk and manage it intelligently. The vast majority of individuals will act responsibly when given some ability to shape their own destiny. Even though it is difficult, a company can get through a transition phase quickly and with grace if top management allows people at all levels to be part of the design process.

The classic mega-merger is given a lot of attention due to the money involved. There is more formality in large mergers. However, to the people impacted, it makes little difference whether the merger is joining two giant corporations or just reorganizing a division within a mid-sized company. The magnitude of the fear will vary depending on the situation. I have seen some department reorganizations that have been incredibly upsetting to people, but it does not always happen that way. In a mega-merger you can be sure that some people will be terrified, in a smaller one, however it is less of a sure thing. The terror of an insecure job is greater than the magnitude of the merger. The confusion of not knowing your job function and having to invent new processes for everything will feel the same whether your check is written by AT&T or a small bank merging with a similar one in another city.

The antidote includes the use of a thorough process, even for a limited reorganization. There is a balance here, and I advocate using the thought processes of a mega-merger to guide the thinking process of smaller deals. The only difference is the time and resources used in the analysis; the checklist should have the same items. Table 4.1 is an example checklist that can be used in a reorganization of any size. The only difference will be the difficulty of getting specific answers. In a small reorganization, the answer may be a sentence, whereas in a mega-merger the analysis may take months and involve numerous people.

Use this list as the basis for discussion with the people impacted. Rank items on a scale of 1 to 5, with 5 being the most critical, and then define the order of importance. Add any additional items at the bottom of the table. The group can identify what resources will be required to answer the question, whether those resources are people, time, or funding. It is helpful to specify the specific plan to accomplish each step as a separate document. Finally, the group might benefit from considering the order in which these questions are answered since some items will need to be nailed down in order to answer other questions.

Table 4.1: Pre-Change Checklist

Item to define	Critical (1–5)	Resources	Order
Is there a compelling case to do this?			
Have we investigated the possibility of doing nothing?			
Has the ideal end state been defined?			
Were the people informed about this early?			
Will this increase or compromise trust?			
Is the business case documented and robust?			
Do we have the resources (internal/external)?			
Have we considered the impact on the customers during transition?			
Are there any legal restrictions?			

Is there a union involved in either group?			
Do we have enough bench strength?			
How will we train people in the transition?			
Are we clear on compensation and benefits?			
Can we keep key people onboard?			
Are we doing this at the right time?			
How will we dispose of excess materials?			
Have we defined the impact on the community?			
Other:			

Summary

Change can produce a good result if it is properly planned and managed. The key is to maintain trust during the transition because that will make the whole process smoother.

In the next chapter we will discuss a very important ingredient that will help with the trust issue and make the entire process more credible. The idea is to have the top leaders highly visible during the entire process. Unfortunately there is a human tendency for the opposite to happen.

Food for Thought

1. Think of a minute change process that is going on in your world. Can you apply the checklist to that simple change?

2. A checklist for transitions can never be complete. There are always things that can be added. What items would you add to the list?

3. What excuses do organizations use for not involving people earlier in the process? Are these reasons always valid?

Part III:

Tips for the Process

In this section we will look at the main steps in an integration and explore the impact on stakeholders and the business. You will learn tips to improve each part of the process and the best way to keep employees' trust in a time of transition.

5

Avoid Isolation
During the Process

"Remember you don't do anything in isolation."

King Abdullah II

In this chapter you will learn:

- It is easy to become cloistered away and lose touch with reality during the study and design phases.

- Involving people must be done carefully for legal reasons, but it is possible to control leakage.

- Have a integrated team help with the design of the process. This is the best way to maintain or build trust during the reorganization.

- The team can perform all kinds of duties that will save management time and keep the workforce onboard.

Much of the work on a potential change effort occurs with the top executives closed in a room with accountants and lawyers trying to assess valuation and jump through the legal hoops. Usually there is a data room set up for this purpose. The room is off limits to all but the elite. What this accomplishes is polarization with an inside group that is insulated from the struggles of the rest of the company. This group has all the power in the decision-making process, but is clueless about many critical issues. Meanwhile, the non-elite are suffering from debilitating anxiety about what will happen to them, not knowing what is going on in the secret room.

Top managers often act as if they are in a bubble of secret and titillating information about the possibilities of the proposed action. Early conversations are kept strictly inside the bubble. The human element and ideas from the impacted people are not considered at this point. The executives do fully intend to cover all personnel (some call it HR) issues later and determine a communication plan to explain the process and benefits. The problem is that later is often far too late to encourage trust from the people in the organization.

The situation is far more complex if either of the merging groups has union representation, which adds third parties to the negotiation process. The process flow needs to determine when and how to include outside employee representation into the process. This can be a simple check box activity, or it can become a ballgame issue or at least a major stumbling block. Although the central union representative is typically neither a member of the management team, nor of the worker ranks, this person must be kept up to date and understand the direction the negotiations are heading.

It is inevitable that the people leading a business deal will slant the discussions toward their area of expertise. Since reorganization involves serious reconfiguration of the financial structure of the organizations, the financial side normally takes the lead. This configuration is only natural, but it has the effect of compounding the impact on people from the very start. In most cases, people are visualized as falling in line with the plan once the financial details have been struck. This attitude allows executives to determine maximum financial value without understanding how people will respond and therefore underestimates the true costs of integration.

The Pareto Principle states that for any set of items, 20 percent of the items contain 80 percent of the value. This principle holds in early merger talks because the human aspects of the proposed action get less than 20 percent of the attention early on, but they really contain 80 percent of the value to the organization long term. Sensitivity to the human aspects of a change initiative is where trust is won or lost every time. By giving less thought to the human aspects of a merger, a great opportunity to build stake and understanding is squandered. There is a simple antidote to this problem.

Include Employee Advocates in the Discussion

Create a nucleus of individuals with equal power to impact the decisions up front. This group should be represented by people-centered individuals (HR or operations management), financial managers, senior officials, and legal counsel. They should work on all aspects of a proposed action in a balanced approach that considers how and when to include employees as a prime consideration. This policy would set up talks on future organizational changes to ensure success. From the first inkling of a reorganization effort, don't let the accountants and executives be the only parties at the table. The remedy here is more transparency.

Create More Transparency

Letting additional people become more involved in the decisions creates the potential for more ownership by employees. Call on top management to be more visible and accessible on a daily basis. The design team approach would have a diagonal slice of trusted people representing everyone who has a stake in the outcome. Among other things they would have a role in deciding:

- the announcement of the plan
- evaluation of staffing levels
- how to communicate decisions
- how team building will occur
- what cross-training will be done
- the key metrics for the venture
- the plan for resolving differences
- supplier and vendor involvement
- the customer satisfaction plan.

Summary

Preventing isolation is a challenge that takes work to overcome. It requires time and has risk. The more people who are involved in the process, the greater the risk of information leaking out. The benefits of having an advocate for employees working right alongside the financial advocates cannot be overstated. This action will be the best defense against trust loss during the design process and will be a vital group activity during the integration process.

Food for Thought

1. Try to think of at least three other functions that should be handled by the design team.

2. How would you go about selecting members of the team?

3. What precautions would you take to ensure that information about the program does not leak out too soon? How do you define "too soon"?

6

Due Diligence

"Diligence is the mother of good fortune."

Miguel de Cervantes

In this chapter you will learn:

- The human part of the equation is often overlooked in the due diligence process.
- Human assets are just as important as physical assets.
- Using extant data is the most objective way to measure people issues.
- Informal evaluations can quickly assess the caliber of how an organization treats people.

The merger process has a due diligence phase in which the planners and legal team attempt to size up the assets of each company to determine value. This information feeds directly into the negotiation process, so accuracy is crucial. It is common for some form of deception (whether intentional or not) to be going on. The level of deception can never truly be known until several months after the deal. In some cases, the disclosure is mostly forthright with only a few areas where the sellers are bending the truth. In many cases, discussion degenerates into conscious deception or downright fraud. Let's examine why this is the case.

In the United States, businesses operate under the doctrine of caveat emptor, or let the buyer beware. This means the buyer cannot recover damages from the seller for defects on the property that rendered the property unfit for ordinary purposes. The only exception is if the seller actively concealed latent defects or otherwise made material misrepresentations amounting to fraud. The problem with this definition is that what may seem like hiding an ordinary condition to one lawyer might constitute deception to another.

Smart buyers find the right kinds of experts to gather the right data, do the careful research, and ask the numerous carefully worded questions that force disclosure of any flaws or potential time bombs. An excellent attorney or legal firm specializing in a particular type of transaction can ensure that both parties in a deal are protected. Scrutiny must go far beyond the straight accounting issues into other areas that could spell trouble for the organization over time. Unfortunately, many due diligence processes fail to uncover an accurate ledger sheet of human assets. The buying party does not have an accounting sheet of the culture that is about to be purchased. However, it is critical to know this for two reasons. First, if the environment is emotionally bankrupt, the value of human capital being purchased is very low. Second, the subsequent cultural integration will be either hampered or enabled by the human capital in both organizations. Poor valuation going in means numerous nasty surprises down the road.

The intellectual ability and motivation level of the current workforce are substantial parts of an organization's assets. These less-tangible assets are no less important than buildings, physical inventory, and monetary assets. If the population included in the reorganization has habitually been abused by the current management, the buyer is going to inherit these problems once the merger becomes public knowledge. How can a potential buyer accurately assess the level of human related assets?

Written survey assessments of the current population can be tempting, but there is a high probability of a Hawthorne Effect when conducting surveys. A Hawthorne Effect occurs when people change their behavior or input when they know they are being surveyed for a certain reason. This renders the data less valid. The information may show a rosy picture only to have the truth of a sweatshop environment come out after the merger.

The use of extant data is a more objective process. Existing historical records of HR data are collected and benchmarked with other companies of similar size and structure. Data might include:

- wage rates for all levels of employees
- absentee records going back several years to spot trends
- safety incidents and accident rates (OSHA reportable and otherwise)
- turnover rates and length of service trends
- reports of disciplinary actions
- union grievances and other labor relations data
- manager turnover and tenure information
- training records including the number of training hours per employee per year
- the communications plan of the organization (both internal and external)

- performance appraisal information and trends separated by individual leaders
- historical employee satisfaction surveys
- productivity levels benchmarked against the best companies in the industry
- records from the employee suggestion box.

The data should be analyzed over time where possible to pick up historical norms and patterns. Also, the data should be sorted by the supervisor. Most human performance levels are greatly influenced by the skill of the immediate supervisor. You might pick up one area where there is excellent morale and productivity in the group, but very low figures for an adjacent group working under a different boss. Knowing the average figures for human performance by area can reveal very helpful information.

For example, suppose the average employee satisfaction for all departments in a factory is 75 percent, but there is one department that consistently has around 45 percent satisfaction. There are three different supervisors in this department, and they all score significantly lower on than average for all supervisors in the plant. You might conclude that it is worth looking into the history of the department manager to see if there is some pattern of abuse by this manager. If you were negotiating to purchase this factory, it would be helpful to have this kind of detail, because it shows a possible need for some change in personnel at the management level.

The use of extant data is much more difficult for a seller to disguise because the data are available and verifiable. If some of the metrics show alarming trends, these can be used as levers to investigate further with focus groups or individual interviews. The important thing is that the buyer needs to spend as much time and energy developing a profile of the human assets of a proposed acquisition or merger partner as with its physical and product portfolios. It is also important to collect data about customers, suppliers, and other external partners. Mining social media makes customer data easier to obtain.

Another way to evaluate the value of human capital in an organization is by observation. This takes particularly skilled individuals who can wander around the shop floor to pick up data over an extended period or have private discussions with current employees. If the right people are doing the evaluation, existing employee problems will surface. Of course, many employees will feign happiness for the sake of helping to get a better deal, but a good interviewer will be evaluating body language in order to pick up any bias. Trust is a major factor in how readily people will share how they feel. If people are afraid of retribution, they will tell the interviewer what they think she wants to hear. If there is a high trust environment, then more accurate data will be gathered. Excellent interviewers will be able to pick up on a high fear situation quickly. Likewise, if there is high trust, it will be obvious.

On the following page is a form that can be used in interviews to determine how human potential is being captured by the current organization. This form is best administered by an outside resource rather than a current supervision because if there is abuse, the incumbent manager is part of the problem. The results of this evaluation will become part of the data that are used in the negotiation process.

Table 6.1: Culture Factors for Due Diligence

	Importance (L, M, H)	Agreement (1–10)
We understand and live by the values of this organization.		
Strategies and tactics are clearly articulated.		
I agree with the goals of this organization.		
I trust my supervisor.		
I know what I am supposed to do at work.		
My manager empowers me by bringing out my best effort.		
This is a happy place to work.		
I enjoy working with my peers.		
My contributions here are appreciated.		
I am compensated fairly for my work.		
There is some stress, but it is manageable.		
There is time to recharge my batteries.		
We are told what is going on. I feel in the loop.		
I have been well trained.		
I like working for my boss.		
Other:		

This is a simplified form. Most consultants have their own version that they prefer to use. The idea is to pay attention to this kind of information in the due diligence process. These methods will take some effort, but they form a basis for knowing how well the human capacity of an organization is being nurtured in the current environment. That is a critical issue to understand before going into any kind of organizational change initiative.

Food for Thought

1. Observe people at your workplace. Try to identify their enthusiasm by watching their body language and listening to what they say.

2. What role does trust play in an engaged workforce?

3. Is it possible to spot extreme employee unrest before there is a major blow up? What would you look for?

7

Negotiation

〜〜〜〜〜

"Everything is negotiable. Whether or not the negotiation is easy is another thing."

Carrie Fisher

In the chapter you will learn:

- M&A negotiations are very tricky because the parties need to work well together after the deal is struck.

- Negotiations are never standard. There is always a twist or turn to anticipate.

- There are several basic principles that apply to every negotiation. Learn them and use them.

- Learn the tactics and countermeasures that are often used in a negotiation. You will come out much better when you are aware of the rules of the game.

After the due diligence process is completed, if it looks like the reorganization effort will go forward, a negotiation phase is planned. Usually this is a formal event that takes place off-site and is very carefully orchestrated by professionals who specialize in making deals. It is an interesting dichotomy, because on one hand, each party wants to get the best deal possible out of the negotiation for the shareholders, yet the two parties will be on the same side once the integration begins.

Both parties must walk a very fine line between getting the maximum value out of the negotiated financial deal, and maintaining the highest level of trust and respect possible so the merged entity gets off on a solid footing. Preparation is the key to success, but this is even more important in the case of a merger because of the delicate balance of needs.

For example, if you are purchasing a house, you can afford to be hardnosed during the negotiation because if the other party is upset with you, it does not affect you. There is normally no contact after the sale and closing. This is not the case in a M&A situation. The negotiation is just one phase, and the pivotal phases for success come during the integration. The plan for the negotiation process must take this into account, so the negotiated deal leaves a firm foundation to build on.

The atmosphere in negotiation meetings varies widely depending on the circumstances of the deal and the temperament of the parties involved. Meetings are often long for a variety of reasons. First, the use of time in any negotiation is a common ploy, and fatigue makes people want to get something over with just to get out of there—concessions come more readily when people are tired. Second, meetings are long because of the expense and business disruption of having two management teams off-site, so they use as much of the day as possible. Third, the issue of stamina becomes part of the negotiating strategy.

I recall one situation where a CEO was contemplating the purchase of a diversified company with offices all over the world. The selling CEO wanted to impress the buying CEO with how things work in the fast lane, so he arranged a trip around the world to visit every site as part of the due diligence. The idea was to exhaust the buying CEO so that he would cave in during the negotiation. The seller even took along two assistants so they could relieve each other and have an unfair advantage. The ploy totally backfired. I was present when the selling CEO came back from the week-long journey. He looked completely exhausted. His comment was, "Where did they get that guy? He ran rings around us and always came up smiling. We were absolutely dead on our feet." So, what was intended as a ploy to gain the advantage turned into a liability for the seller. The secret was that the buying CEO was a master at sleeping on airplanes and in taxis. He could get good quality sleep on every leg of the trip, while all three of the opponents could only sleep a little and did not get much rest for the entire week.

I recall another situation where one party tried to gain leverage using time, and that also backfired. This was a negotiation for a product line made in Japan. The principal, I'll call him Don, flew over from the United States to negotiate a deal and was scheduled to stay for a week. He was outnumbered, of course, and was a guest on their home turf. That was a big advantage for the Japanese, who decided to put time pressure on Don. They dragged their feet and brought up all kinds of small issues to avoid the financial negotiations until the final day. The Japanese host said they found out which flight my friend was going to take so they could get him to the Narita Airport on time, but they actually got the flight information to know when Don would be getting anxious to close the deal and head home. At around 10 a.m., the Japanese host asked for a major price concession and stated, "We have been talking now for five days, and it is time for you to show some flexibility. Besides, we have to get going within an hour to get you to Narita on time."

Don did a masterful reversal when he said, "Oh, let's not rush this deal. It is too important; I'm prepared to stay for another week, if necessary, so we can get this right." All of a sudden the time pressure was on the other side. The Japanese host had been entertaining Don every night, and it would take him almost two hours to get home after he dropped Don off at his hotel. He was exhausted and wanted my friend out of his hair, yet Don claimed he was willing to stay for an additional week. The Japanese host quickly made a huge concession, and Don still stayed the extra week to hammer out the details.

The use of time in the negotiation process is always important, and good negotiators find ways to leverage this important consideration. At the end of the day, the negotiation rests on human beings who have physical and mental limitations. Expert negotiators will exploit these limitations.

Negotiating Principles

There are five basic negotiating principles that you need to know and practice in order to do well. They may seem obvious, but you would be surprised how many anxious CEOs violate one or more of these principles and pay a big price at the negotiating table.

You Have More Power Than You Think

It is a normal to underestimate one's own power in a negotiation and overvalue the opponent's power. You feel that kind of pressure when you go to purchase a car. You only do it once every few years, and you are up against a salesman who does it every day. That is pretty intimidating. The antidote is to list the pressures that the salesman is under, and you will realize that there is significant leverage going in your direction. You just need to be alert to the other negotiating tactics in order to get a fair deal. In a M&A case, you need to lay out the pressure points for the other party in great detail. The more you know about your future partner, the better you can balance the hard and soft side of the discussions to get a fair deal without creating unnecessary acrimony.

Have a Plan

Don't try to wing it. I am amazed by how many people go into a negotiation with a vague idea of what they will offer and then see what reaction they get. That is not the way to get the best deal. If you sweat out the details and go in with a specific strategy you will do better. For example, one strategy might be to keep part of the organization out of the negotiations at first then add it to the mix as a leverage point later in the process if you need to break a log jam. That sort of strategy is developed ahead of time and should not be attempted on the fly.

Leave Room for a Concession

We know this rule in our personal life, but many business leaders forget to use it in negotiations. You should aim higher than you are willing to accept. You never know what will happen, and it is much easier to lower your terms than it is to raise them. Leave enough room so you can make a nice concession at the very end to close the deal, but still be in good shape overall.

Seek Win-Win Deals

A deal will not occur unless both parties are convinced that they are better off with the deal than without it. That does not mean each party is happy with the deal, just that he or she is better off. Always search for win-win solutions in a negotiation. It adds to the quality of trust and enhances the chance of making a deal. Never belittle or embarrass your opponent, after the announcement you will be working together trying to make the venture successful.

Have a Walk-Away Position

Know how much you are willing to give and have a firm level where you are willing to walk away from the deal. This puts the other party on notice that there is a limit to your flexibility. When you reach your walk-away position, it is important to actually close off the negotiation, or your credibility and self-respect will be trashed.

Tactics and Countermeasures

It is critical for each side to have a professional negotiator on their team. They are familiar with all the tactics and countermeasures that come up when negotiating. If the other side has a great negotiator and your CEO wants to represent the company himself, you will get clobbered if he has not been trained in negotiating. There are scores of useful tactics that are used in negotiations, and your team needs to spot them and know the countermeasure to avoid being a victim.

The Bogy

This is a tactic where one party claims to only have a certain amount of a resource available. The resource is usually money, but it could be time, material, or intellectual property. The ploy is that you make a convincing show that you have only so much of the scarce resource, when it would be possible to find more, if necessary. The most frequent bogy is the budget. One person will say, "We just do not have any more in the budget." That is supposed to end the conversation, but a skilled negotiator will know a countermeasure and say something like. "I understand the budget does not have any more room for this item, but a budget is something you have created, and there is flexibility to move funds from one year to the next or from one category to another." The countermeasure when faced with a bogy is to immediately challenge the validity of it. A bogy can almost always be thwarted if you put it under the microscope.

Good Guy/Bad Guy

This ploy is from the technique used in police interrogations. The bad cop brow beats the suspect hour after hour trying to break him down. Eventually the bad cop leaves for some made-up reason and a good cop comes in with kindness and a reasonable approach. Often the good cop is able to get a confession where the bad cop could not. Auto dealers use this approach extensively.

In an M&A negotiation, the roles to be played would be orchestrated in advance by each team but carefully guarded. Good guy/bad guy usually works, even if both parties are aware of the charade, because the dialog gives both parties a reasonable explanation for why a concession was needed. The countermeasure for good guy/bad guy is to actually name the tactic and call them on it. Say something like, "Oh we are not going to play good guy/bad guy here, are we?"

Anger

This is a theatrical technique where one party pretends to be so annoyed that they physically walk out of the meeting leaving the opposing team with nobody to talk to. This type of tactic is used frequently in labor relations. It is used less frequently in M&A negotiations because it can create a lot of animosity. The antidote for this is to just allow the walk out and not get upset by it. Recognize it is a ruse. They will be back, and you can resume where you left off. If you do not get rattled by the theatrics, then your opponent will realize they create minimal power (or even lose power) over you by playing head games.

Splitting the Difference

You should try to bait the other party into offering to split the difference first. Then you have their concession recorded first and you can make only a partial concession in reply. This is such a common ploy that it is rarely tried in sophisticated M&A negotiations, although it does often work in personal negotiations.

Silence Works

In most cultures, silence becomes uncomfortable if it goes on for more than 20 seconds. Good negotiators use extended periods of silence to put pressure on the other side to make a concession. If someone tries to use the silent treatment on you, just stare back at him or her for as long as it takes. Call their bluff. Another startling countermeasure when someone is using silence is to raise the stakes, rather than make a concession, after a period of long silence. It is totally unexpected, so it has power.

For an easy personal example that is readily translated to the business world, suppose after a heated debate the person who wants to purchase your car has gotten you to offer it for $800—$400 below your asking price. The buyer pulls the silent ploy and just clams up, hoping for a further concession. You should stop talking as well. You wait him out until he breaks the silence with, "How about giving it to me for $750?" You stun the buyer with, "Well I have been sitting here thinking about it,

and I really cannot offer it at $800 at all. I was wrong. The price is $900."
You have reversed a former concession, so the potential buyer no longer believes there is any opportunity to get you below $800.

The Nibble

This tactic is a request at the last second to throw in something of low value once a big ticket item has been purchased. For example, when getting ready to pay for a $400 dollar suit, you might say, "You will be including a nice tie in the deal, right?" The countermeasure is to simply say, "No, the ties are $25, but we have them on sale this week for $20 each. How many would you like?"

Summary

This is not an exhaustive treatment of negotiating tactics or countermeasures. There are specific courses and numerous books on the topic. One book that I like is *Give and Take* by Chester Karrass. Tactics and countermeasures will surely be in play in some fashion during any negotiation. Make sure someone on your team is well trained as a negotiator.

The deal will go back and forth on one issue after another. Each concession does not stand alone. After giving in on point 6 of a contract, it is fair game to go back to point 3, which was already agreed upon yesterday, and say it is now unacceptable based on the flexibility shown in point 6.

One interesting aspect of a negotiation is that it is never really over. I know one organization that wears down the opposition for many days, then comes to full agreement, even signing the papers. The next morning they come up with a change in conditions and indicate that the contract is void, and they have to reopen it. Such a tactic shows low integrity and lowers the chances for a fruitful relationship. It definitely compromises trust, but some people will try to get away with it.

We need to remember that after the acrimony of the negotiation, these two entities still need to work together on the terms of the agreement and the all-important integration process. If the hatred is so intense that one party is bent on getting even, then it will play out in unexpected ways over time. Great negotiators have a credo of fairness that they will not violate just to get the last bit of cash out of a deal. Reason: When a person feels taken advantage of, he will find some way to get even. Maintaining trust and the perception of integrity is more important than the last bit of cash in any deal.

Ultimately negotiations come down to use of power. There are numerous methods and individual styles. Sometimes the ploy is a trap or a lie, but other times it is a sincere effort to get a reasonable deal for both parties. It is a spectrum, and you can find all varieties of honest and dishonest negotiators. For trust to exist after the deal, it is important to only deal with negotiators with the highest integrity.

Food for Thought

1. Recall the last time you bought a car and identify the main negotiation tactics you used to get the best price. Could you have done even better? How?

2. Try using silence in a negotiation and see if it works out for you.

8

Announcing the Merger

"The danger of the web is that you can go from idea to public announcement in under 10 minutes."

Seth Godin

In this chapter you will learn:

- The announcement phase is brief but very important to the future health of the combined organization.
- Handle the challenge as an opportunity rather than a chore. With the right attitude, you can use the announcement phase as a springboard for the culture that you desire.
- Do not just try to "wing it" on the announcement. Have a solid plan and lots of help with it.

Planning the Announcement

The announcement of the merger is a critical point in the process. I think of it as a fulcrum, or even a birth. It is often the culmination of months of challenging work, and it creates a juncture with the start of the integration process. Many organizations do not put enough thought and planning into this phase. Let's pick apart this critical moment from the point of view of several stakeholders and offer ideas that can help make it more successful.

Tell Shareholders First

The owners of both entities must be told first because they will be involved in the transfer of wealth. They are the beneficiaries of the deal or they may feel like they have lost ground. You need to reassure the owners that the deal is sound and that it is a good deal for them.

Tell Employees Early

Make sure the employees are the next to be informed after the shareholders (or almost simultaneously), before the media, customers, and suppliers if possible. Putting employees first models the transparency that is so important for trust.

The announcement of a merger rarely comes as a surprise to employees. They have been aware of things going on and are smart enough to figure out there is some kind of ownership change in the works. They just do not know the details or understand how the new configuration will affect them personally and this causes anxiety. Up to this point, the information could not be shared publicly for legal reasons. Now that the information can be shared, employees need to see that they are first in line.

Get Help With PR

There may be a major influx of media attention around the announcement. Some groups try to field all the questions themselves and get tripped up because of all the other things that need to be done simultaneously. A professional PR firm will help you craft the announcement for various purposes and even help with the dissemination. They can also be helpful if there is negative backlash either from reporters or the social networks.

Send a Special Message to Customers

It is easy for customers to feel abandoned in the flurry of communication about the merger. You need to prepare a message of continuity and better customer service specifically aimed at giving your customers the perception of worth and stability. You will enhance value if you think of this as a significant opportunity to connect with customers in a different and powerful way. If you let customers find out the details from the media, you will be missing a chance to create a stronger bond.

Remember the Community

People in the communities of both companies will be vitally interested in the announcement. Make sure you state your intentions without being too crude. I recall one organization that bought out a small tech firm in another city. Their message was that "We see no problem bringing them on board in just a few weeks." That told the community where the acquired firm was located that the jobs would be going away soon. That announcement was not the best way to handle a transition in terms of future reputation. It got the acquisition off on a particularly sour note and there was significant avoidable damage done.

Suppliers Are Wondering Too

The two companies' suppliers and vendors have a vested interest in continuity. The announcement will often feel like a threat to these important partners. A carefully worded statement about the value of strategic partnerships and that there will be an enhanced role for the best partners will provide a positive vision as the evaluation and potential consolidation of vendors takes place. The best firms will stand to gain while those that have issues will often get pruned. That is great news for the groups who earn the right to continue as partners in a larger enterprise.

Consider the Timing

The timing of a major announcement is important. Putting out news of a major reorganization on a Friday afternoon is a bad idea. The rumors and misinformation will become viral over the weekend and damage control will be needed the following week. The best day for an announcement is Tuesday, because people have settled in for the week, and there is still plenty of time to meet with small groups face to face before the weekend. If the organization has a shift structure, it is important for executives to carve out the time to meet with the off shifts along with the day shift.

Be Ready

Consult the checklist in Table 8.1 before announcing of a merger, acquisition, or major reorganization.

Table 8.1: Before the Announcement

Likely questions (You need to have responses for each of the three audiences.)	Employees and staff	Customers and vendors	Media and community
What will the timing be for making the announcements?			
What will the company be called?			
What is the organization structure?			
Will either location be closed or moved?			
What is the impact on wages and benefits short and long term?			
When will decisions on staffing be announced?			
What is the training program for employees?			
Are there any new reporting structures?			
How often will we hear about progress on the integration?			
What infrastructure needs to be in place to handle responses to the announcement?			
Are there any special considerations or precautions to be taken?			
Other:			

What to Say

The basic idea in an announcement is to tell people as much as you can at the moment, and give them a timing statement for the things that are yet to be decided. Do not duck the issue of who will stay and who will leave. That is the most pressing topic on everyone's mind. If the decisions on personnel have not even started when the announcement is made, how can you maintain or build trust in that situation? Here are some tips:

- **Tell the truth.** Since there is no longer a need for secrecy tell people what will be happening as candidly as you can. If you have set some targets for workforce size, you can share them, but give yourself some flexibility by giving a range rather than an exact number.

- **Describe the process.** Tell employees the exact steps you will be taking over the next period of time. Include the layout of needed skills, criteria for selection, who will be involved in the process, and what to expect in general.

- **Promise updates, then deliver.** People do not like to be in a vacuum. Deliver frequent updates at least three times a week on the process and give ample opportunity for questions. Make sure all questions get answered promptly. Do not use smoke-screens or tricky legal language in the responses. That kind of approach will cause even more angst.

- **Give timing information.** Once people are aware of the process going on, most of them are focusing on the date when the pruning will be done. Tell them a date and stick to it unless there is a good reason to extend it. People are waiting for information about their future. If you do need to make an extension, make sure it is only once. Do not wait for months and leave people hanging.

- **Continue enhanced communication.** The need for more information and communication between management and employees does not go away once the staffing decisions have been made. During the integration process, aim to double the normal amount of time for communications. This means more time just wandering the floor to keep a pulse on rumors. It also means being more alert to inaccurate information on social media.

Summary

The announcement of a merger is a special opportunity, but it can be the beginning of a long downward spiral if not handled well. It is important to use the opportunity to demonstrate transparency and deference for the people who will make the organization successful in the future. Take the time to plan the roll out well, and make yourself available to answer questions and deal with special needs as they come up.

In the next chapter we will cover the role of the human resources department. The employees there have been busy throughout the processes of research, due diligence, and negotiations. After the announcement they will be preparing for the integration. When it comes time to do the downsizing, there will likely be some in HR. The next chapter will offer some insights into the importance of this special group to the entire process, along with tips and precautions.

Food for Thought

1. What mistakes have you seen made when managers announce a merger?

2. What additional resources might you call in to help with this phase beyond what is mentioned in the text?

9

The Key Role of
Human Resources

～～～～～～～

*"The best way to be productive is to have a great team.
So I spend more time than most CEOs on human resources.
That's 20 percent of my week."*

Kevin P. Ryan

In this chapter you will learn:

- HR becomes the control point in the reorganization process.
- The load on the HR department more than doubles in times of transition.
- The decisions made by HR will have a direct impact on the subsequent trust levels.
- Beware of cutting HR resources too soon.

In any reorganization, one of the most taxed groups is the human resources department. The success of the venture and the health of the resulting organization are highly dependent on the skill and dedication of the combined HR unit. HR is in a funny position, because they do not constitute the direct line management of the organization, but the policies invented and administered by HR have a huge impact on trust within an organization.

It would be tempting to downsize the HR function early in the merger process, since duplicate staff functions are generally trimmed as a result of any merger. However, HR needs to provide a strong leadership role in the reorganization process. HR has many different and critical roles during the integration. Having to perform them all flawlessly during an extended transition with reduced staff would not work well for the business. If there is a weak HR group, the transition is not likely to work out.

HR Roles for Reorganization

Here is a sampling of new roles to be played by HR during reorganization. These are over and above the normal HR roles in steady state times.

Provide Data During Research and Due Diligence

HR is generally the repository of extant data that will be used in the negotiation process. The staff is called upon to organize and analyze mountains of data on people and make some sense of the mess. They also must maintain the database in the future, so they must migrate both systems onto a common platform during the integration phase. This aspect alone is a monumental undertaking

Advocate for the People Process During Negotiations

The process leading up to a merger can take months or even years. During that time, both organizations are expected to run at top performance, because each one is being scrutinized for valuation purposes. The HR staff must keep all elements of the planned merger under wraps for legal reasons while simultaneously analyzing the potential impact of the merger.

Create Uniform Policies

HR policies and procedures need to be shaped to the new reality. This involves working with key stakeholders in both units to sort out a steady stream of issues, like flex work plans, vacation plans, salary rationalization, benefits alignment, movement of people, communication systems, performance appraisals, dress code, the progressive counseling system, safety procedures, and numerous other critical operational decisions. In these decisions, HR is a pivotal player with management and the workforce.

HR also acts as the record keeper so that the impact of decisions can be traced and the organization can demonstrate compliance with all laws. The latter issue becomes a huge burden in times where the policies are being changed by governmental or other mandates.

Work to Blend the Cultures

Historically, when mergers fail to produce expected results, it is often due to the inability of the cultures to blend into a homogeneous hybrid culture. A classic example of this was the Daimler-Chrysler merger discussed earlier, where the two cultures never did merge. HR must take the lead, bringing in the appropriate resources (such as teambuilding experts or leadership improvement consultants) early in the integration to keep the two cultures from becoming calcified and rigid. It is during the integration process that dysfunctional and even childish behaviors may become evident at all levels. The HR department becomes the control point for the organization for all these cultural issues. They are the facilitators of culture.

Sort Through Downsizings and Keep Morale High

Inherent in most mergers is the ability to trim back on redundant functions in staff and production groups. This is a critical issue for any merger process. HR must ensure that any downsizing activity is done fairly and with the appropriate sensitivity to the welfare of impacted individuals. When reductions do occur, it is often the people staying who feel like the true losers, because they need to survive in a working world that sometimes seems untenable. Usually HR is involved in trying to prop up sagging morale before, during, and after downsizing efforts.

Advocate for Transparency

Information dissemination during a merger process is a critical element, and HR is usually involved in the roll out of information. The ultimate level of trust in the merged group will be closely linked to the level of transparency people witness during the various phases. HR takes on many roles from advisor to top management to conduit for information to designing communication processes and being a sounding board for feedback.

HR personnel need to guard against being too conservative on the issue of transparency. Normally when top executives want to divulge a certain piece of information, it is the HR representative who questions whether it is better to withhold the information. HR acts like a lawyer in these situations. They can see the risks and downsides to communicating information too soon. They have to be cautious because if things spiral out of control, they will have to work harder to unscramble the mess. For example, HR will usually vote to postpone the downsizing announcement because some employees may do inappropriate things. HR wants to shorten the time between the announcement of a layoff and when those impacted leave the premises. That lowers the risk, but keeping a layoff under wraps for too long has a devastating impact on morale and trust, so HR has to balance two opposing forces to get it right.

Handle Training Integration

The learning management systems (LMS) of the two entities are likely to be different. Each group will want to hang onto their familiar way of scheduling and tracking the training activities of their people. Major battles can erupt over the work required to convert from one LMS to another. The victor is perceived to have won over the group that needs to retool, however hard feelings over this issue can last for years. Sometimes a blend of the two systems works well where both groups are called upon to modify their past patterns with no winners or losers.

Minimize Distractions

What is the name of the merged unit? If both names of the separate units are in the new name, which one comes first? Which CEO is perceived to be the top dog and which one has to get used to being second in command or needs to leave? What will the logo look like? Who gets to reside in the prime real estate? What outside training group is selected? On and on, the issues seem endless, and what appear to be rather straightforward decisions quickly become emotionally and politically charged. In all these decisions HR plays a role of a key resource and source of information on the impact.

Summary

It is common in a merger for both parties to feel beleaguered and put out by the other party. It is hard to maintain objectivity and fairness when groups feel they are under attack. What might seem like a fair split to top managers may feel incredibly lopsided to both groups at the lower levels.

The workload of HR from first inkling to full integration is much more difficult than what will occur in a steady state operation. That is why it is important to not downsize any seemingly redundant HR resources until full integration and stability have been achieved. It may be wiser to have a slight increase in staff in order to do the job right. These expenses should be included in the original ROI calculations.

Food for Thought

1. Write down some additional key roles played by the HR group.

2. What would happen if the top HR manager decides to leave in the middle of the process?

3. If each organization has a very strong HR manager, would you let both of them stay or select one to be the new HR manager?

4. Would you consider some outside help with integrating some of the benefits work?

10

Managing the Impact

~~~~~~~~~~~~~~~~

*"The only limit to your impact is your
imagination and commitment."*

Tony Robbins

In this chapter you will learn:

- The key to a successful transition period is adequate planning before the announcement.

- Move the process along smartly, but do not rush the changes. It is a delicate balance.

- Do the pruning very carefully. Avoid the mega cutback approach.

- Place special emphasis on the systems changes. You might want extra resources onboard for this critical work.

A typical merger or substantial organizational change takes the better part of a year or even longer from inception to complete integration. Many of the large bank mergers over the past decade have taken two to three years to complete. During the transition, few people in either organization are happy.

This chapter deals with the upset in business. We will discuss many situations that occur on a daily basis and offer suggestions to move the process along without sacrificing the quality of the integration.

During the consolidation process, nervous employees may start looking around for more stable employment. Logic tells us that the most employable people (the ones with the most talent) are going to find alternate employment more easily than the dregs of the organization. A protracted period of integration can result in the best people leaving while the poor performers end up staying. The key ingredient to expeditious assimilation is the degree of trust that is maintained during the process. Without trust there are many false starts and blind alleys that drag out the effort and sap energy.

The issue of how fast to consolidate staff positions is a delicate one. On one side, everyone is on pins and needles before the decisions on staffing and the selections are done. This is a time of low productivity and poor customer service. Once the major wave of layoffs occurs, there is a collective sigh of relief, and people become more energized to figure out how to operate in the new organization. On the flip side, cutting too fast and deep will mean fewer people to do the work while all the turmoil is going on. If you need to hire new people to keep up the pace, they will have to be trained, creating more chaos. There can also be a major loss of trust and other problems that are associated with cutting too much, too early. However, depending on the corporate culture, it can work. When Apple cut 20 percent of its workforce over a two-week period, it was severe, but it worked for them. In many cases, such cuts would cause a major loss of trust. So what is the right time and right way to make the cutbacks?

I favor a phased approach rather than a massive layoff. Do a lot of cross training among people and keep them busy with thinking about the future. Go slow on the downsizings until things begin to stabilize. Let attrition and defections accomplish the bulk of the pruning with lower pain. Offer voluntary separations and incentives for those who want to leave, but be sure to let the critical resources know they are essential.

Table 10.1: Consequences of Speed

	Move very slowly	Move quickly
Advantages	• Time to consider options carefully • People can adjust with less shock	• Ability to hang on to best people • Get it over with so people can lower their stress level
Disadvantages	• You tend to lose the best resources • Hanging on to some redundant staff too long	• You may cut too deep and regret it • Not much time to train replacements

Aim to slowly downsize redundant resources over a period of three to six months. Stretching it out longer will not improve the situation and acting sooner may be premature.

Another determinant of speed is how quickly the new systems can be integrated. There will be extensive work to get the IT systems and supply chain methods on the same platform. During this integration period people in both camps will be quite frustrated. Things don't work as well as people wish they would, and they have to do extra work just to get a quality product out.

One technique is to have a parallel process where the new system is operating in tandem with the old systems for a while. Just continue as if there were two entities, but have the new system run in a beta mode for at least a couple months to work out the kinks. Then throw the switch to have the new system in control while the older systems crank in the background as a safety net in case there are more problems. Keep this overlap time to a short duration because it is a lot of extra work, but it could prevent a catastrophic failure of the supply chain.

The other insurance policy for IT systems is to have a manual workaround for emergency situations. This is a good idea for a business anyway, because the computers do not always operate, but the organization must be able to run continuously.

The personnel process is another area of turmoil in the transition. Every HR related policy must be examined and a decision needs to be made to go with the policy of Unit A or the policy of Unit B, or perhaps a new policy for the joint group is the best option. Make these decisions with care and design them as early as possible. It is not necessary to transition all systems at once. Take the most important one, like payroll, and attack it first. Postpone the integration of lesser important issues, like parking plans, to a later time. Set a priority order for HR systems integration and do not get ahead of the plan unless there is a good reason to do so. The HR staff will be swamped with personnel issues beyond the system upgrades during the transition, so it is wise to go at a reasonable pace.

Move things along as quickly as the people can absorb and learn the changes, but guard against going too fast, so people don't become confused and make a lot of costly errors. I am not advocating making hasty and dangerous decisions in order to get it done. Rather, I am proposing intensive planning about all aspects of the consolidation before the start. The people involved should be allowed to participate in the planning process so they have an opportunity to contribute. More specific and concrete plans are better for integration. Then, once the consolidation is formally announced, the time to return to a fully functioning organization will be much shorter. Yes, it will be painful, but the work upfront makes that pain more manageable.

In the next chapter, we deal with keeping the right people. If you end up with an inadequate workforce it will hamper your chances for success or even survival. People have an opportunity to leave at their own discretion. It is impossible to hang on to an employee who really wants to leave, so learning how to keep the employees who are vital to your success is important.

Food for Thought

1. How can you tell if you are moving too fast? What are the key symptoms?

2. How would you let certain people know they are considered key resources for the future?

11

Keeping the Right People

~~~~~~~~~~

The actions around staffing decisions will determine the success or failure of the entire effort more than any other single factor.

In this chapter you will learn:

- Keeping the best employees is critical, but they are the ones who can get jobs most easily.

- Financial incentives to stay need to be applied with great care. They can backfire.

- The lowest performers can cause problems during the transition. Be vigilant.

- How the downsizings occur will govern the level of trust going forward.

Whenever two groups merge, there is a change in personnel and positions. Typically there are fewer slots after a merger, so some staff are let go. Often, this winnowing process goes all the way to the top of the organization. A huge conundrum for the health of the business is how to keep the right people on the bus and get the wrong people off the bus. This chapter outlines the challenge and offers methods that management can use to keep more of the best people.

During the final planning phase for the transition, before the official announcement, it is a best practice to evaluate staffing needs because at the announcement people will immediately ask for information about layoffs. Your response cannot be "We haven't figured that out yet."

Some organizations wait until after the announcement to make plans for staff sizing because they feel a need to have more people involved in these decisions. This is dangerous too because it adds to the uncertainty and lack of trust. People not only worry about whether they personally will have a job, but they also have a legitimate worry about the quality of leadership and survivability of the business. People cannot trust a leader who comes out and says, "I don't have the answers to your questions today, but we will be working on it—trust me." Forget it! A statement like that will cause many capable individuals to start dusting off their resumes.

During the assimilation process there is normally an evaluation period where executives figure out the more specific staffing decisions, such as the number of people in each function. Then they seek to fill those slots with the best qualified individuals from the talent pool of the combined groups. After the selection process, the remaining people will receive some painful but expected news. How this phase is conducted will have a more significant impact on trust than anything else that goes on during the reorganization. The actions around staffing decisions will determine the success or failure of the entire effort more than any other single factor.

The real ballgame happens long before the official selection process. Top management had better do the right things then or some of the most talented individuals will not be in the crowd when the selection process begins. The managers of both groups may believe they are in control of staffing when really they are not, and many of their actions during the due diligence phase can actually cause some of the best people to seek more secure jobs.

Long before the announcement of a merger is made, people in both camps are at least vaguely aware that something is happening because rumors of a major discontinuity have been circulating for months. People in both organizations are justifiably nervous. Even the highest performing individuals are unnerved enough to start questioning their longevity, at least to themselves.

The very best and most marketable individuals have a good chance to land comparable or superior positions in more stable organizations, so they may start looking for alternatives long before any forced ranking of staff takes place. By being proactive, they often have alternate employment secured by the time the announcement of the merger is finally made public.

On the flip side, the least talented people, or those who are lazy or have interpersonal issues recognize that they are vulnerable in the ranking process. They also realize they are not going to find many opportunities on the outside, so they hunker down and prepare to defend themselves through legitimate or fraudulent tactics. Their objective is to stay employed if at all possible and they will do whatever is necessary to ensure that when the music stops, they are near an empty chair. Their strategy may involve some unfair pushing and shoving.

One of the first actions top management should take is to identify the few critical people they need to be around in the merged organization. When I say first, I mean long before the action becomes common knowledge. These people need to be informed that their place in the new order is assured, and it will mean a better existence for them. Of course, that is a tall order, because the truth is that there are far too many unknowns in the months running up to a merger to legitimately assure anyone of anything. It is important to do what you can here.

In this situation, some kind of contingent bonus may be helpful. Stock options are often used as a tool because payment can be substantial, but it only occurs when the organization itself thrives. People will think twice about leaving a $100K job to go to a new organization if they can see a potential $1M payout in stock options if the merger is a huge success.

The downside of any bonus incentive is that of fairness. Basically, top management is singling out a few of the best people (in their opinion) to entice to stay. That will unnerve the mass of people in the middle who believe they are contributing just as much to the organization as the favored individuals, but are not receiving an incentive to stay. That sends a chilling signal that impacts motivation and productivity for the majority of people at the very time when the due diligence process is examining the numbers for valuation purposes. This problem can be mitigated if the performance evaluation system in place can single out the top 10 percent of individuals, so any retention incentive can be thought of as an additional reward for high performance.

Monetary incentives are not the only tool managers can use to allow key individuals to know they are valued during a merger. Simply having a candid discussion about the situation with individuals can go a long way toward having them want to stay on the team. It is always a good strategy to let the best people know they are valued, but the benefit of doing so is amplified significantly during the months before a merger announcement.

Another idea is to have key people serve on planning groups that are charged with assembling data for the due diligence process or in developing the communication plan. When individuals are included in active work to accomplish the reorganization, they instinctively know there will be a place for them once the dust settles. Keeping the best people busy working toward the future is the best way to keep them from looking for other more secure work.

The vast majority of workers are not super stars, yet they are presumably all trained dependable workers, and you will need most of them in the new configuration. How can we keep these people from getting itchy to look elsewhere? The truth is you cannot save the entire group. You can only communicate the path forward as openly and calmly as possible, and hope that by having solid information on the business going forward, people will be less nervous about having future employment.

The final category is the dregs of the workforce. These people are the ones you would like off the bus at the end of the process. One strategy is to identify the bottom 10 percent and let them go. If you end up with too few people, at least you have made sure the ones you kept are the high performance individuals.

For the poor performers, I think a frank discussion about the future on an individual basis is prudent. They need to know that there will be cutbacks, and they need to be reminded that there have been some issues with their performance in the past. The problem may be poor quality work, attendance issues, interpersonal conflict, bad attitude, or a combination of all these things. If the performance appraisal process has been working, these individuals will already know they are at risk. The key thing is to let these people know they are in jeopardy and that you are not going to tolerate any monkey business while the process sorts out.

Since the slackers have nothing to lose, they may try some disruptive actions to keep their job. These actions can take various forms and supervision needs to be alert to head these things off before they surface. One challenging ploy is for the employee in question to feign an accident. He may trip over a forklift left partially in the aisle (on purpose) and wrench his back severely (or may claim a back injury when there really is none).

Another ploy is to figure out a way that firing this particular person would be discriminatory. Whatever angle the employee can think up is likely to surface, because the person has nothing to lose.

You may think that the possibility of a future employer getting a poor reference would be a deterrent, but you would be wrong. This individual is already well aware that you would not give a good recommendation, so there really is nothing to lose if he tries some trickery to gain leverage. Keep a close eye on people who are at the margin and be prepared to walk them to the gate anytime they get out of line. They are not productive, they are usually a drain on the emotional state of the group, and they are capable of doing some damage through sabotage.

I have seen examples of people who knew they would be cut trying to make some of the stars look bad by sabotaging their work. The motive here is usually jealousy rather than self-preservation, so be alert to this type of childish behavior. Most people will not stoop to this kind of thing, but you can find a few rotten apples in almost any barrel.

Having the right people on the bus following a merger is the most critical consideration governing the success of the effort. How you go about doing that will impact the level of trust in the organization going forward. I believe it is essential for top management to take steps to ensure the best people stay and do so with honesty and integrity. These actions need to be accomplished during the conceptual phase of a merger, not while the formal integration process is unfolding.

When preparing for integration, there are two things going on at once. First, the old businesses are continuing to operate as if nothing is happening. Second, a new combined company is forming. In the next chapter we examine how looking at organizational change from a systems point of view can be quite helpful.

Food for Thought

1. What other methods could you use to retain the best people?

2. How can you tell if a poorly performing worker is a danger to the organization?

3. How would you go about building higher trust if there is no ability to tell people what the staffing level will be when the announcement is made?

12

Systems View

~~~~~~~~

"I believe that our very survival depends upon us becoming better systems thinkers."

Margaret J. Wheatley

In this chapter you will learn:

- System thinking tools can be helpful in the reorganization process.
- Only use the tools if you know how to use them correctly.

Classic systems thinking can help organizations through the transition after the reorganization announcement is made. In this chapter we will take a look at a few classic systems thinking tools and apply them to the common transition problems.

Systems thinking is using different tools designed to observe a process from different angles through special lenses. The techniques are useful in any corporate environment because they allow leaders to understand how to change the process without suffering negative repercussions. It is particularly useful in a merger or acquisition because there is so much turmoil that it is hard to see the true process. Systems thinking allows leaders to see the process amidst the chaos and to intelligently design future changes that will work.

We will look at five of the more powerful systems thinking tools and give an example to show how each one might be applied in a merger.

Input/Output Analysis

The technique of input/output analysis is a simple way to get an over-view of transition requirements. Draw a box around the phenomenon you wish to study, then:

- List all the things that feed into the box.
- Identify what you expect to get out of the box.
- Document the environment—called the task environment—in which the box is operating.

For reorganizations, the box is the merger activities. The inputs are defined by the two separate organizations before the integration. This list includes all the people, skills, inventory, physical assets, customers, and so on. Everything going into the action needs to be identified. Coming out of the box is the steady state integrated culture after all of the transition activities are done. Creating this visualization shown in Figure 12.1, is quite helpful because it is not always obvious what the final outcome should look like. Doing this analysis helps crisp up the objectives for the actual integration. Next, document the external environment for the new organization. That environment includes governmental rules, the cultures of the countries, transportation networks, data handling methods, suppliers, competition, and all other external factors that influence the organization.

Figure 12.1: Input/Output Process

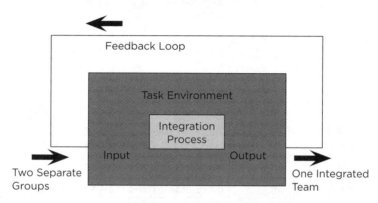

Now that all of this work is completed, focus the energy on the box itself. What steps, in what order, need to occur to have the inputs in this environment produce the result we desire? Analyzing the inside of the box gives a glimpse into what transition activity needs to happen. It forms a crude roadmap for the entire effort.

Input/output analysis can consume a lot of time, but it is fantastic for being able to spot the big picture and not get lost in the details. You can do a simplified version in a one-hour meeting that will give a bird's-eye view of the entire process, and then you can follow up with more detail later.

For a large company, you will want to use the analysis to identify the integration steps for the different areas separately. As an example, your worksheet might include brainstorming in the areas shown in Table 12.1.

Table 12.1: Example Integration Worksheet

Area	Steps to Full Integration
Manufacturing Process	Train operators, remove excess staff, recertify ISO 9000
Research and Development	Assemble technology portfolio, determine areas of focus for next year, rationalize research equipment inventory
Marketing and Sales	Redraw the territory to rationalize, generate combined compensation plan, downsize staff if possible
Customer Support	Consolidate to one location, train on new product lines, automate manual processes
Quality and Engineering	Write new quality procedures, reduce redundant personnel, migrate to 100 percent CAD system for design
Billing and Accounts Receivable	Issue new credit terms, automate billing cycle, create self-directed teams
Staff and Management	Reduce staff by 40 percent, reorganize to have one organization chart, design uniform leadership training

The input/output technique is helpful at any time during the integration process. What I recommend is that you do a thorough job at the start, and then revisit the chart quarterly to check on progress and update it. The chart becomes like a map of the high level actions that are going on, and it is particularly useful for communicating the entire effort to people in the organization when they get lost in the details. Employees need to internalize the strategy.

Strategy

Systems thinking relies on a solid strategic plan. If you don't know where you are going with the integration, then your chances of getting there are pretty slim. In most cases, organizations have developed strategic plans, but now it is necessary to come up with a strategy for the integration. Think of it as a strategy within a strategy.

In developing strategies, most organizations err on the side of too much detail. I prefer a high level view first, and then decide if a more granular plan is needed. Often it is not, but there will be cases where both a bird's-eye view of the strategy and a more detailed operational plan are helpful.

You can create a high level strategic plan in as little as 10 hours. I have seen groups struggle with strategic plans for two years, only to have the resulting tome be too heavy to lift, let alone execute. Try to have the entire plan on two sides of a single sheet of paper. On one side you document the purpose, values, vision, mission, and behaviors. On the reverse side you list the strategies, tactics, and measures. I prefer to limit any organization to a maximum of five key strategies at any point in time. The benefit of doing strategic work is to focus attention on the few vital key result areas. If you are trying to juggle 15 strategies, you cannot have the proper focus. The single-sheet strategy looks at the integrated strategy from 30,000 feet. To view more operational detail, you would provide documentation of each strategy with specific tactics and action items required to achieve them.

One key distinction that trips up many groups and causes confusion is the difference between strategies and tactics. Strategies are broad statements of what you are trying to accomplish. For example, if you have a vision to create an integrated manufacturing facility out of several different component factories located in different countries, we might have a strategy to "combine operations under one roof." Tactics are statements of how we will accomplish the strategy. In this case two tactics might be "purchase a building" and "move existing equipment."

Metrics are specific indicators that allow us to see our progress accomplishing the strategies. In the example, one logical metric might be the "percent of production equipment that has been relocated." Another key metric might be the "percent of workers who are trained on the new process."

The most important part is not the creation of a strategy document. You now need to enroll the entire population to understand and support the various items of strategy. This process is called *alignment* and the end result is that everyone in the combined organization:

- understands the strategy
- sees his or her part in accomplishing the strategy
- becomes excited about the future vision
- has the ability to see how the pieces fit into an integrated plan.

Input/output analysis is an element of the strategic plan process. Another common element of developing a strategy is the SWOT analysis, which stands for strengths, weaknesses, opportunities, and threats.

SWOT Analysis

SWOT is a way to document the existing processes in an organized way. You document the strengths of the organization, or in the case of a merger, the strengths of each group. Then you consider the weaknesses of each group. Sometimes these elements are determined as part of the due diligence process.

Documenting strengths and weaknesses is like looking at each part of the integrated organization through a microscope. You are examining the elements to see where there are natural skills and where there are gaps to be filled. This analysis is quite helpful for identifying ways to transplant key people in order to balance out talent.

The second half of SWOT looks at the opportunities and threats. This part of the process looks at the world through a telescope from the vantage point of the existing structure. Threats are usually easier to identify than the opportunities. Managers can simply document the areas of vulnerability, but the trick is to dream a little bit about what the competition might be up to in the next year or two. That takes some facilitation skills, so it is wise to have a trained expert in the strategic process help the group make the best use of time.

The opportunities part is where the most leverage is uncovered. I like to use a kind of trick with groups when documenting opportunities. We do the classic brainstorming of opportunities. What comes out are a bunch of ideas that people have already been kicking around. Let's say a group of eight managers comes up with 40 opportunities in their 30-minute brainstorm. Then I challenge the group to at least double the number of ideas on the list without dropping any of the brainstorming rules (the most important being to suspend judgment until a later time).

In this second effort to document possible opportunities, the real gems spill out. People have already exhausted all the easy ideas, so challenging the group to double the list forces a much deeper creativity and amazing ideas start to surface. If you are rigorous with the suspension of judgment, then SWOT analysis will become a rich source of ideas that will lead to significant opportunities for the merged group to tackle.

Winnowing ideas down to a manageable set requires some kind of a sorting method. There are several useful techniques you can use. A quick one is the Pareto voting technique, where people select the top 20 percent of items they think have the best potential from a long list of possible ideas. When you combine the Pareto votes of all members you will have a good list of the best ideas.

Force Field Analysis

Force field analysis is where you document the equilibrium of the current conditions and then identify what forces are causing it. The technique is particularly valuable for identifying leverage points for potential actions and then analyzing the forces that are working to enable the change process versus those that are restricting it.

To use this method, you state the equilibrium that exists at the present time with respect to the change effort see Figure 12.2. Now identify all the things that are enabling that condition to exist on the right, showing arrows pushing on the equilibrium state trying to move it to the left.

Figure 12.2: Force Field Analysis

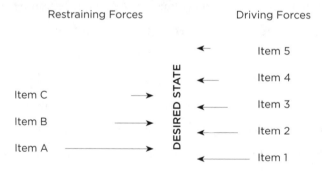

Next, list all the forces that are restraining the equilibrium from moving to the left. These are shown as arrows trying to push the process to the right. Along the way make crude estimates of the magnitude of the driving and restraining forces.

This may be hard to visualize, so let me give a specific example. Suppose the desired state is an integrated customer service operation in one location. Table 12.2 lists the driving and restraining forces in a hypothetical analysis giving the magnitude of each force on a scale of 1 (low) to 5 (high).

Table 12.2: Forces Maintaining Current Customer Service

Driving Forces	Restraining Force	Weight
Streamline operations and communication		4
Increase number of agents		3
Use common training		2
	Have two buildings	5
	Resistance to new equipment	2
	Inadequate parking facilities	2
	What to call the integrated team	1

Now we are in a position to advance the change effort. We can do that by either enhancing one or more of the driving forces, by reducing one or more of the restraining forces, or by doing both. In this case, perhaps we would try to increase the importance of the driving force of a common training platform in order to improve acceptance. Also, since the existence of two facilities is a significant restraining force, we might reduce that with a strategy to move the operations into a single building in three stages and lease out the remaining parts of the unused facility until we can sell the building outright.

By having a visual idea of how forces are impacting the current equilibrium, it is easy to select things to work on that will have the most impact. Each situation is unique and the actual analysis will depend on the situation. It is important to have a trained facilitator apply these tools, so people do not become bogged down by the methodology and stay at a strategic and helpful level.

Lewin's Radical Change Model

Curt Lewin envisioned a model that is helpful in making change programs work. The idea is to have processes in place that are fixed or "frozen" in a configuration before the change. These processes are unfrozen to allow movements of any part. Finally the new processes are documented and refrozen in the new configuration.

For example, let's envision that we are trying to combine two separate groups, accounts payable and accounts receivable, into a single group to improve overall efficiency. The original state is where information is coming into each group separately and processed independently for action. The process has been "frozen" in this configuration historically. Now we "unfreeze" the situation to allow both groups to receive information on both types of transactions and to log the appropriate information into a common accounting ledger. That condition would be rather chaotic, so we combine activities and streamline the process in one physical area. Then the process is "refrozen" as a combined function.

One could envision the entire reorganization process going through this three-step process, but it is more helpful to put each piece of the change through the model and then add up the pieces. That keeps the analysis relatively simple to manage.

Using the Five Models

These are the five conventional systems thinking models that are helpful for conceptualizing any change process. I include them in this book as examples of how systems tools can be quite useful in a reorganization. One precaution is that the tools should only be used by people who are schooled in their use.

Systems Thinking Example

Let's look at an example of how strategic tools and a systems view led the successful reorganization of Ford. For Ford's reorganization, CEO Alan Mulally had mapped out a simple schematic depicting the key decisions that had to be made at each stage in Ford's value chain, along with the infrastructure required to execute them effectively. Every week, he and his team tracked their progress in making and executing these decisions. They divested non-core brands such as Aston Martin, Jaguar, Land Rover, and Volvo; reduced the number of production platforms; and began consolidating suppliers and dealers.

Along the way, they decided to reorganize the company, moving from a structure based on regional business units to a global matrix of functions and geographies. This new structure enabled Ford's leadership team to make some of those critical decisions better and faster—creating global car platforms, which had been painfully difficult under the old structure. Ford still faces challenges, of course, but so far Mulally's approach has helped Ford ride out the hurricane lashing the global auto industry and turn in stronger performance than its U.S. competitors.

Here we see that using sound strategic preparation and astute organizational work to solve specific issues was the key to success. Not only was the reorganization well planned with specific goals, but it was executed with precision and patience and that effort paid off. Reorganizations need this kind of organized approach to be successful.

Food for Thought

1. What other systems thinking tools would you recommend for a merger or acquisition?

2. What are the dangers of getting involved with systems thinking during a reorganization?

Part IV:
Integration Tips

In this section we will look at what leaders can do to ensure a smooth transition. In particular we will focus on the importance of culture during transition and the best way to downsize without burning out good employees. The section ends with a chapter on accountability, the cornerstone of a trusting work environment.

13

Building Culture in Transition

"You can design and create, and build the most
wonderful place in the world. But it takes people
to make the dream a reality."

Walt Disney

In this chapter you will learn:

- Real culture includes people and relationships, not just corporate norms and habits.
- Eight ways to improve the culture of a group.
- Case studies help but do not prepare students adequately.

During integration, the organizations involved are not going to be in a steady state. The level of turmoil might be compared to navigating a boat down a series of rapids. At times just keeping afloat and running with the current is the reality. Other times there will be adequate resources and time to think about strategy. This chapter walks through deployment of resources in a way that allows an overarching strategy to coexist with the fierce paddling required to avoid smashing onto the rocks.

Considering all stakeholders is essential to form a pattern of trust during the process. If trust is compromised, then all other aspects of the integration are going to take longer and be more problematical. One might think of trust as the life jackets that are worn throughout the process so there is maximum potential for reaching the end safely.

What Is Culture?

One way to think about culture is how the organization collectively acts or reacts given a set of circumstances. Here are a few examples of how a culture might be defined for an organization:

- tolerance for risk (conservative, bold, or even reckless)
- flexibility (rigid and slow or fast and agile)
- level of teamwork (mostly individuals working together or self-directed teams)
- problem solving (data driven or gut feel approach)
- use of technology (old school or progressive)
- investment mentality (big spenders or tight with money)
- diversity (mostly a mono culture of people who "fit in" or highly diverse on all dimensions, age, gender, race, nationality, religion, background, and so on).

The culture of an organization is made up of numerous elements, and how it is experienced depends on one's vantage point. For example, a production employee views the culture as something that provides him or her with safety, a decent living, and good working conditions. The customers will view the culture as a collection of functions that provide a good quality product at the right time for the right price. A shareholder would view the culture as a set of activities and assets that are aligned to create a return on her investment.

Culture is an intangible phenomenon, but it is essential to be able to portray the culture accurately, because that is how people experience the organization. The culture gives an organization life so that it has the ability to perform as needed. It tells us what to expect under any given set of circumstances. Unfortunately culture is often viewed as a narrow set of parameters, as if there were only one legitimate viewpoint.

I know a CEO who has a mid-sized business. In order to expand customer coverage, she was contemplating the acquisition of another group that was roughly the same size. She really liked the fit of the two businesses and was convinced it was a wise business move. The initial due diligence did not reveal any skeletons in the closet. She talked with all of the managers and was comfortable that there was a good fit in terms of personality. The financial part of the deal was acceptable to both parties.

She decided to take one more step before the final commitment. She took a week to visit the operation personally and chat with the employees one on one. A different and disturbing picture began to emerge. She realized after a couple days of discussions that the two cultures would never be able to work well together. The operating styles were so different that it would take years of effort to blend the cultures. She backed out of the deal. As she told me the story later, she said, "I really wanted to do that deal. I thought it would be smart. But after getting to know the culture, I realized it would have been the worst mistake I could have ever made. It would have killed us."

When contemplating a deal with another group, you must consider the operating culture and understand it firsthand to determine fit.

There is no right or wrong when creating a culture. There is no single integration design that works for all major change activities. Each case is unique, but we can follow and customize broad guidelines. We can also learn from history where things either worked well or failed. Several years ago I generated a list that distilled definitions of culture using several different MBA textbooks from different universities. That list included:

- physical structure
- language and symbols
- rituals, ceremonies, gossip, and jokes
- stories, legends, and heroes
- beliefs
- communication patterns
- values and norms
- assumptions and measures
- reinforcement and recognition
- policies and procedures.

These items go a long way toward defining the culture of an organization, but I believe they fall short, because they fail to include the emotions of the people and the dynamics of their relationships with one another. After all, organizations are comprised of people at all levels interacting in a social structure for a purpose.

Here is an extension of the list to include human factors:

- trust levels
- opportunity for career growth
- personal safety
- attitudes and relationship dynamics
- employee satisfaction.

Table 13.1: Corporate Culture Evaluation

	1	2	3	4	5
What is the level of trust within the organization?					
To what extent do people have the opportunity to grow?					
How safe and secure do people feel?					
How high is the respect between management and workers?					
How well do people treat others at the same level, above, or below?					
How much do people generally feel like winners at work?					
How inclusive is the culture?					
What is the level of reinforcement or punishment?					
How much are managers viewed as enablers?					
How acceptable is the turnover rate?					
What is the level of satisfaction of people in the organization?					
How much can people "speak their truth" without fear of reprisal?					
How well do people follow the rules?					
How engaged is the workforce?					

Use Table 13.1 to do an environmental scan of both groups prior to the due diligence phase. This information will be your baseline to form some idea of what the true culture is in each organization. It can also be used to judge progress at various times during the integration process.

The answers to these questions are not absolute, and each person who rates them will have a slightly different set of answers. It is important to have a cross-functional team from both organizations provide the information, so any bias can be factored out. It is common for there to be a bias toward the higher numbers as you go higher in the organization, because upper management usually thinks things are better than the people on the front lines do.

These questions may be difficult to answer in cultures where games are played and people don't deal in straightforward ways. In a low trust environment, it is hard to discuss trust because people are afraid of the consequences of telling the truth.

To get an unbiased response, each person giving the input must truly believe the survey is anonymous. The easiest way to do this is to have a paper copy of the form and a drop box. Stay away from electronic distribution because people will suspect it can be traced.

Building the Right Culture

What can leaders do to ensure that the right culture is built and people have a sense of purpose and meaning in their work? Here are eight approaches that have been used by successful leaders.

Have High Ethical and Moral Standards

Operate from a set of shared values that unites the two cultures and make sure people know why those values are important. It has to start with the leaders. The essence of values needs to be implanted in the hearts, minds, and behaviors of everyone. A plaque on the wall does not make for good values. People living up to their standards makes for good values and creates an environment where people can trust each other and their leaders.

Operate With High Emotional Intelligence

The ability to work well with people is critical during times of change. Without emotional intelligence leaders do not have the skill to lead change and transform intentions into meaning. Leaders with low emotional intelligence also have the most significant blind spots in how they are perceived by other people, as documented by Daniel Goleman (1994).

Build Trust

Trust is the glue that holds people together in a framework of positive purpose. Without trust, we are just playing games with each other, hoping to get through the day unscathed. The most significant way leaders help create trust in transition is by rewarding candor, which means not punishing people for speaking their truth. Most leaders find it difficult to reward candor, but it is the heart of great leadership, as documented by Warren Bennis in *Transparency*. Trust is also enabled by a clear vision and shared values, as described by Bob and Gregg Vanourek in *Triple Crown Leadership*.

Create a Positive Vision of the Future

Vision is critical during integration, because without it people cling to the past and see no sense of direction in their work. If people have a common goal that is communicated well, then it is possible for them to support each other and get excited about the future. Monthly newsletters and occasional town hall meetings do not constitute adequate communication. People must feel informed every day. Having a positive vision of the future and being able to communicate it well enables the change process to be more effective.

Lead Change Well

Change processes are in play in every organization daily, yet most leaders struggle with them. Using a change model can help people deal with the challenges of constantly changing conditions. One example is the grief counseling process, where leaders help people cope with the four phases of change: anticipation, ending, transition, and beginning. People will rise to a challenge if it is properly presented and managed. Challenges as part of a change process are different from demands to perform at levels beyond reason, which lead to resentment and burnout. Properly designed challenges can help people find meaning in their work and in their new business environment.

Build High Performing Teams

A new sense of purpose is enhanced if there is a kind of peer cohesion brought on by good teamwork. Great teams derive an adrenaline rush from achieving results despite high goals. Foster togetherness in teams so people will relate to their tasks instinctively. High performing teams need a common goal, trust in team members, and good leadership. This is even more important during times of change. Strong teams help build enthusiasm and morale. One danger in a merger is that you can have strong insular teams in both organizations, which tends to hinder the integration. Teams take on a tribal atmosphere due to having gone through the stages of formation, storming, and norming. Teams emerge with a kind of parochial thinking that leads to silos of protectionism. In a merger, it is particularly important to be alert to silo thinking and take steps to break it down. One effective technique is to transplant some members from one team to the corresponding team in the other half of the organization. If done carefully, this cross-pollinating can break down the walls between teams rather quickly.

Build Morale the Right Way

There are right and wrong ways to think about morale and motivation. The key is to think of motivation as an outcome of the culture. The level of morale among people at any point in time is a function of the collective culture in the organization. You do not create motivation with a program, it is an outcome of the work you do to create a healthy culture.

Recognize and Celebrate Excellence

Reinforcement is the most powerful tool leaders have for changing behavior. Leaders need to learn how to reinforce well and avoid reinforcement mistakes that are easy to make. For example:

- Do not apply the same reinforcement techniques to all individuals or situations.
- Avoid overusing trinkets like t-shirts or hats.
- Make sure the recognition is reinforcing for each individual.
- Ensure fairness when reinforcing individuals or groups, especially in a merger.

Summary

Most of this sounds like common sense. Unfortunately, it is not common practice in many groups, which contributes to apathy in organizations and hinders integration efforts. To have people rise to their potential you need a strong culture. When two cultures are merging or changing and the composite culture is not well-defined, these steps will help the integrating teams find common ground. Focus on the concepts outlined in this chapter to see a remarkable transformation in your organization.

The culture forms the foundation for everything that goes on in an organization. It is essential to understand and manage it. That is true for any organization at any time in history, but it is particularly relevant for groups that are trying to merge or somehow integrate. Each entity will have a unique culture that is a montage of all the variables. Not all of the elements of culture will be the same or even be compatible. It is this clash of cultures that causes serious problems during every transition. It often leads to the complete failure of a merger, but it could also lead to some creative solutions that could increase diversity and benefit everyone. Making the right calls throughout the integration is the ultimate test for the leaders of the organization.

Food for Thought

1. Why do some MBA programs fail to see the glaring omission of the impact of culture in reorganizations, mergers, and acquisitions?

2. The list of ways to improve a culture may be incomplete for your situation. Can you think of two or three other items that should have been on the list? Can you see a pattern or generalization in your response?

14

Living the Values

"A people that values its privileges above its principles soon loses both."

Dwight D. Eisenhower

In this chapter you will learn:

- The value "people are our most important asset" is extremely difficult to defend if you want to have your actions match your words. Be careful before adopting that language as a value. Can you really act that way?

- Behaviors that would support this value are not commonly seen in corporations, but many smaller companies are getting the message.

Many organizations say, "People are our most important asset." It stands to reason why this should be the case. People are usually the biggest expense item in the budget of an organization. They hold the intellectual capital of the organization. They research future streams of products. They produce the current products or services. They work with the suppliers and vendors who make production possible. They sell those products. They administer the business and keep things working financially. Organizations would be myopic to not recognize that people really are their most important asset.

In a merger, you may have both companies espousing that employees are their most important asset, but only one organization comes close to acting that way. Often it is the case that neither organization is adhering to their values very well, so people in the merged entity are left to wonder what the underpinnings of the organization are going to be. Go to the websites of both companies and compare their lists of values. It will help expose cultural differences.

A best practice is to sort out the values of the merged organization before the announcement, so the employees can understand the intentions of top executives as they struggle to act consistently with them. Unfortunately, few leaders act as if they believe people are the most important asset, so the value statement reflects a major hypocrisy. This pretense is amplified in merger situations where people rightfully see themselves as expendable commodities rather than precious assets. This is a powerful trust buster.

The problem is that in the dreaming phase, executives write value statements that are ignored in the execution phase. If leaders espouse the value of their people they need to act that way at all times. In reorganizations, usually one of the goals is to be more efficient, which means fewer people. The truth is, "*some* of our people are our most valuable asset."

It is in the daily actions of managers and leaders at all levels that the hypocrisy of the statement shines like a neon sign. In conference rooms, computer notes, offices, private discussions, decision meetings, town hall meetings, and every possible form of interaction, managers are dealing with the business of transition and ignoring the plaque in the lobby. If management is not behaving consistently with the value, why should employees believe them?

What would mergers involving organizations that really do believe people are the most valuable asset look like? Here are some ideas:

- Managers would take the time to interact with most employees on most days. They would not be cloistered in conference rooms, deciding whether or not to tell people about the progress of the cultural integration.

- Communication would be intended to engage people, not to spin the latest information in an effort to avoid a revolt.

- People would have a sense that upper management really wants them to rise to their potential. There would be a greater emphasis on cross training.

- Recognition for good work would be spontaneous and light hearted, instead of an obligation to be performed begrudgingly with insincerity. Recognition would include both parts of the merged organization equally.

- Flexibility would be evident when employees have personal issues or family matters to deal with instead of maintaining strict discipline or showing preferential treatment.

- Trust would be abundantly evident in all matters rather trying to document all forms of behavior not following strict guidelines.

- CEOs would seek to have a better balance between their own salaries and those of the workers. They would not tolerate a huge gap in pay.

- Ethical decisions would be made because it is just good business, rather than to comply with regulations.

- Cultural centers would be constructed where all employees could learn to appreciate each other and embrace the culture of the other group.

- Organizations would welcome social networking and transparency rather than try to seek ways to restrict these trends out of fear of being exposed.

- Managers would spend less energy trying to explain financial performance to Wall Street and more energy trying to improve the cultural integration of their organizations.
- Leaders at all levels would learn the value of praising people who express a concern about inconsistencies, building higher trust on a daily basis by reinforcing candor.

It is possible to accomplish this kind of environment where building trust is the key. People judge leaders by what they do, rather than what they say, so the challenge here is to consistently model the values.

The people value is a wonderful ideal. We need to encourage all leaders to make their actions and policies consistent with their words. Some organizations have been able to accomplish that to a large degree. These groups have become the best companies to work for in America.

In a merger or acquisition, be particularly sensitive to any inconsistency in the values statements and get them sorted out as early as possible. You cannot build a successful integrated culture on two sets of values.

Now that we have a vision of the culture we want at the end of the process, how do we integrate the two cultures to make it reality?

Food for Thought

1. Compare the behaviors in your organization with the list. Do you see any of these behaviors being practiced?

2. What alternative wording might be more appropriate to describe the importance of people in a values statement?

3. If you were coaching a leader in an organization who said that people were his number one asset, what would you tell him or her?

15

Integrating Two Cultures

"Some people think that doctors and nurses can put scrambled eggs back into the shell."

Dorothy Canfield Fisher

In this chapter you will learn:

- The road to integration is not smooth, so expect some setbacks along the way.
- Always model the behavior you want the rest of the organization to show.
- Have lots of celebrations and praise to encourage people.
- Do the tough stuff with courage and dignity for the individuals impacted. This is a great time to show a little class.

Companies rely on teams. Getting teams to work well within one company is hard enough, but getting two sets of teams from two different companies to work together can seem downright impossible. This chapter deals with blending two cultures into a single high performing team. The challenges are immense. Achieving a stable culture where people are at least supportive, if not enthusiastically driving a singular mindset, is the most significant challenge for most change efforts.

Even when the action is described as a merger of equals, one group will feel they have been "taken over" by the other. Curiously, in many instances, both groups feel they have been taken over, because employees in each group will need to modify procedures to accomplish the union. Usually, one of the parties is assumed to be in charge, so it is the other party that needs to endure the bulk of the changes.

Ideas to Improve Team Integration

Lack of trust and genuine animosity can lead to resistance when blending the two groups into one. People will appear to agree, but will instead subversively undermine the other group however possible. This kind of "us versus them" thinking can go on for years, if allowed. So what actions can management take to mitigate the schism and promote unity? Here are some ideas that can help.

Plan a Phased Cultural Integration

Trying to accomplish a full integration in one giant leap is as dumb as climbing one of the world's highest peaks in a single day. It is just too overwhelming. When groups climb a major mountain, they establish a base camp where they can get their bearings, practice on the terrain, get acclimated to the altitude, and do some team building for the challenge ahead. They usually hire an experienced Sherpa to help them improve the odds. Exactly the same progression should be used in organizational change.

1. Let people become acclimated to the idea of a new entity. Give them the guidance of experienced facilitators, let them

"practice" by trying out new procedures, and do a lot of teambuilding.

2. Establish a base camp where it is safe to take the next step. Then establish a camp 1 about a third of the way toward integration. For example, you might start the integration by combining the billing groups and leave the rest of the organization in the old configuration. Later you might combine the manufacturing groups into a single entity.

3. Identify which groups are going to integrate first and concentrate on making them successful. Then establish a second step where the bulk of the areas are integrated, but there are still some areas operating in the old way.

This phased approach accomplishes many things including:

- making people less overwhelmed
- presenting a successful integration in one area as proof before other groups tackle the job
- allowing some breathers for the individuals involved, as well as the Sherpa.

Start Early

Do not let doubt and suspicion grow. Work quickly after the merger is announced to have combined teambuilding activities. Openly promote good team spirit and put some money into developing a mutually supportive culture. Good teamwork is not rocket science, but it does not occur naturally either. Unity requires an investment of time and money.

Have Zero Tolerance for Silo Thinking

Human beings will try to get along at all times. Set the expectation that people will at all times try to get along. Monitor the wording in notes and conversations carefully and call people out when they put down the other group. This monitoring needs to include body language. Often eye rolling or other expressions give away mistrust.

Blend the Populations as Much as Possible

Move key individuals from Group A near their counterparts from Group B. Do this with care and it will not take long for the individual cultures to be homogenized. Sometimes the transplanting process is unpopular, but it is an important part of the integration process.

Use the Strategic Process

It is important to have a common vision and goals. If the former groups have goals that are not perfectly aligned, then behaviors are going to support parochial thinking. When conflicts arise, check to see if the goals are really common or if the support is only on the surface.

Reward Good Teamwork

Seek out examples of groups working well together and promote them as model behaviors. Verbal and written reinforcement from the top will help a lot. You might consider giving an award for outstanding integration behavior. People should be encouraged in every way to act and think in an integrated way. Having the incentive plans pay out only if both units perform seamlessly can encourage this.

Model Integrated Behavior

Often we see animosity and lack of trust at the highest levels, so it is only natural for this behavior to pervade the rest of the organization. People will pick up on the tiny clues in wording and body language. Leaders need to walk the talk on mutual respect.

Co-Locate Groups Where Possible

Remote geography tends to polarize any organization. Moving at least some of the merged group under the same roof will help to reduce suspicion. If cohabitation is cost prohibitive, it is helpful to have frequent joint meetings, especially at the start of the integration process. Modern technology allows for online video interaction, which while not as effective as being together in person, helps groups get to know each other better than emails or phone calls.

Benchmark Other Organizations

Select one or two companies that have done a great job of blending cultures and send a fact finding team with representatives from both groups to identify best practices. This team can learn cooperation best practices to help spread unity through the entire company.

Align Metrics With Joint Behavior

Make sure the metrics are not contributing to silo thinking. If the goals are aligned for joint performance, have the metrics reinforce behaviors that accomplish the goals. Often, well-intentioned metrics actually drive activity that opposes the intended result. One way to test for this is to ask, "What if someone pushes this measure to the extreme? Will that still produce the result we want?"

Weed Out People Who Cannot Adjust

A certain percentage of the population will find the change too difficult. Identify these individuals and help them find roles in some other organization. It will help both the merger process and the individual. On the flip side, identify the champions of integration early and reward them with more exposure and control.

Summary

The road to a fully functioning integrated culture can be long and frustrating. By following the ideas given in this chapter, an organization can speed up the process and help employees feel a sense of belonging to the new organization.

Do not promise that everything will go smoothly. Groups will make some progress and then slip back due to an incident or personal disagreement. Expect this and do not allow people to become disillusioned or discouraged every time there is a setback. The best attitude for managers to have is: "We recognize the road from where we were to where we are going is not going to be a straight line. There will be setbacks. We are not going to come unglued when they happen, but we will try to learn from our missteps and move back on track as quickly as possible."

Consider a constructive award process to encourage inclusive behavior. Give out a Champion of the Cause award each month to recognize the individual or group that is doing a great job modeling excellent integrated behavior.

Changing an entire culture is a lot of work, and the best way to move steadily toward the goal is to make people feel good when they are doing the right thing. Never miss a chance to say "good job" and "thank you."

Food for Thought

1. Do you think it would be helpful to develop a road map for the integration?

2. How could you turn an integration problem into a great learning experience?

3. If people resist being transplanted to the other side of the new organization, how can you make it more tolerable?

16

Process Design Phases
of Transition

*"To improve is to change, so to be perfect is
to have changed often."*

Winston Churchill

In this chapter you will learn:

- People generally resist change, yet change is inherent in any reorganization effort.
- To use a nine-step model to helping change efforts be successful.
- How a four-step grief counseling model can shorten the recovery time significantly.

It seems like there are more management books on how to lead change than any other topic. One key theme in these books is that people resist change. In my consulting practice, I occasionally run into a group of people who really love change, but they are the exception to the rule.

To experience a demonstration of the phenomenon as you are reading this book, fold your hands completely by interlocking your fingers and thumbs. Now reverse the order of your thumbs. That is how change feels.

Any change process represents a series of challenges. This chapter looks at the process through phases. Different actions are important at different points in the process, but the whole effort integrates into a large system view. It is important for stakeholders to understand where they are in the change process and what they can expect to happen. There are stages that employees go through that are perfectly normal. For example, early in the transition, there is often denial. Later on, one can expect some form of bargaining and some hostility. Understand that these phases are typical and try to work through the transition with a framework that avoids panic when typical behavioral patterns emerge. Using a structured process for dealing with the phases of change allows leaders to enhance trust while navigating choppy waters.

Some people need to be trained on functions from the other side of the organization. Use an organized approach to the training that is logical and explain that logic. Lay out the plan and make it visible so people can relate to the current training as part of a bigger picture. The sad truth is that most change programs produce negligible results despite a lot of invested time and money. Successful change leaders do the following things well.

Demonstrate the Need for Change

Some mountain climbers freeze to death each year because they fail to recognize a change in weather until it is too late. If they go out on a blustery day when the temperature is subzero, they will immediately go back to base camp and put on more layers. But if they start out with bright sunshine and little wind, they feel pretty good. They start to climb and do not notice the weather changing little by little. They acclimate to the changing conditions and rationalize that even though it feels a bit colder, they were fine before, so they can tough it out. Before long, hyperthermia sets in and they need to take a little break. They lie down, go to sleep, and never wake up. The leader's role would be like that of a Sherpa who brings a dose of reality to the process and does not let the climbers go beyond their limits.

In a merger, the need for change is obvious, because the two organizations were doing somewhat different tasks in the past. Integration requires a lot of change to be successful, but in less dramatic reorganizations, the need to change may not be so obvious, and this is where the leaders must alert people to the dangerous situation and demonstrate a need for change.

Communicate a Compelling Vision of the Future

A good vision lets everyone in the organization know where they are headed. It needs to be specific enough so people can see their role in making it a reality. It needs to be positive and inspiring so that people feel it is worth the effort (Barker, 1985). Leaders need to paint the picture of a fully integrated entity functioning well in the future.

Build an Environment of Trust

Trust is built or destroyed by leaders as they interact with individuals from both of the merging units and build trust-based relationships with each of them. Trust between people is built on every day actions and behaviors large and small that either build trust or break it down. It is a very sensitive system that can be affected even by subconscious thoughts or small gestures. Making small or medium changes is easy, but large increases are rare. Unfortunately, decreases can be large and devastating. All trust can be wiped out with a single action. The typical change initiative is rife with opportunities for this outcome. Leaders need to prevent this by having all their actions consistent with the vision and with what employees hear them say.

A problem arises when people interpret the actions of leaders as incongruent. In most organizations, people are punished in some way if they bring up an inconsistency. In reorganization situations, when tension is high and new leaders are brought in, people shy away from making waves. They need to be encouraged to speak up. In an organization of high trust, leaders reward people for pointing out gaffs because it allows correction or clarification but, more importantly, it fosters additional growth in trust by encouraging open dialog.

Rewarding candor sounds simple, but it rarely occurs. Usually leaders hate to admit mistakes. They believe it weakens their ability to lead and they become defensive when employees push back. This reaction normally backfires and reduces trust in the leader.

The irony is that admitting mistakes is normally an excellent way to increase rather than reduce trust. Unless the mistake is a repeat of a prior error or a stupid one, when a leader admits a mistake it increases respect and trust. Most leaders know this intellectually, but not too many find it easy to do when the opportunity arises. This is a result of ego and the need to avoid shame. Building or rebuilding trust during the integration phase of a change initiative is vital to its success.

A Four-Step Plan to Build Trust

1. Start by laying a firm foundation with your team. Identify the shared values of your business along with a clear vision, behavior expectations, and a strategic plan.

2. Encourage people to tell you any time they believe your actions are not congruent with your foundation.

3. Reward them every time they do it, no matter how challenging that is. Make them glad they told you about it, especially if they are from the other part of the organization.

4. Take appropriate corrective action or help people think through the apparent paradox. Be sure to avoid taking a parochial point of view.

This method works because it uses what I call the "I am right" theory. Each of us has a set of beliefs based on everything we have experienced in life. We own these views and truly believe they are right. When another person observes a situation and comes away with a judgment different from ours, we think they must be wrong. Similarly, the ideas from people in the other group are more likely to be suspect.

For example, as a leader, I see my batting average as 100 percent because "I am right." I believe everything done or said is justified and consistent with the vision. If not, I would do something else. In my leadership classes, I hand out a button with those words to all of my students to remind them that we all have this mindset.

The trouble arises when we add other people. In reorganizations, there are many new people, but there hasn't been time to build rapport and suspicion can be an issue. In their eyes my batting average is far from 100 percent. With extreme care, I may be able to achieve 60 to 70 percent, but inevitably I will do something viewed as inconsistent. One of two things can now occur.

First, the other person can say or do nothing. This reaction would normally seem the safer one. There have been previous opportunities to voice a contrary opinion, where this person has felt punished rather than rewarded for voicing a dissenting opinion. It is just not safe to do it. We used to call such episodes CTOs, short for career threatening opportunities. Unfortunately, they occur frequently.

What happens to trust in this situation? It goes down! The person has less trust in me because I appear hypocritical, acting in a manner inconsistent with our mutual values, behaviors, or vision. My trust in him also goes down because my subconscious knows something is wrong, but the other person is silent. If the issue is a substantial one, trust goes down dramatically.

Contrast that result with a scenario where the other person verbalizes the problem immediately, because it is safe to voice a contrary opinion. An environment of trust has been built, so people know this kind of input is welcome.

Here the outlook is much brighter. We can have meaningful dialog on the discontinuity. I can reverse my action with a statement like, "You're right, I didn't think of it that way. I'll reverse my decision. Thanks for pointing that out." Another response could be, "I really appreciate your pointing out the inconsistency. I still believe my decision was correct and can't reverse it. Thank you for having the courage to speak up. Now I know there is an issue. If you have a problem with it, others may as well. Let me explain further why I can't reverse the decision." Either way, the trust level goes up. I have been listening. The other person knows she has been heard and her opinions respected. I know the other person is being honest with me so trust goes up in both directions.

With this approach, you have a powerful correcting force when people believe things aren't right. If something is out of line or they are uncertain about it, they will tell you, enabling modification before much damage is done. Now you have an environment where honest feelings are shared and there are no large trust issues. This kind of environment helps ease the concerns of people roiled by the stresses and uncertainties of transition. People will feel safer with the changes occurring if they feel it is safe to speak. People in your organization will interact with you gladly, spending less time fretting and more energy pursuing the vision. There will also be less gossip and fewer rumors.

Value Different Opinions

The people closest to the work generally have the best solutions. Leaders need to tap into the creative ideas of everyone in the organization for change initiatives to be successful. This also allows people to own the change process rather than perceive it as a management trick to get more work for less money. Leaders will have more knowledge of their own processes, so the ability to really listen to the ideas of people from the other group is a major advantage.

Accept Risk

No progress is made without some kind of risk. As a leader, you need to empower people so they feel free to try and not get squashed if they fail. Tolerate setbacks along the road to success and don't lose faith in the goal. Try to manage risk so the consequences are minor if failure occurs. For example, have a backup plan in place for changes that involve risk. It is important to manage leading indicators in addition to lagging indicators. This automatically reduces risk. For example, tracking monthly sales is an important indicator of health, but you might also track the number of new sales leads generated each month as a leading indicator.

Build a Reinforcing Culture

Many groups struggle in a culture where people hate and try to undermine one another at every turn. They snipe at each other or complain about others to management just to get even. What an awful environment in which to live and work, yet it is far too common, especially when you are trying to join two groups who are suspicious of each other.

Contrast this with a group that builds each other up and delights in each other's successes. These groups have much more fun. They enjoy interacting with their co-workers and are about twice as productive! You see them together outside work for social events and there are even close family-type relationships in evidence.

As a leader, you want to develop this second kind of atmosphere, but how can it happen in an environment that has been forced together, experienced upheaval, and perhaps an uneasy union? A good place to start is with yourself. Make sure you are practicing positive reinforcement in a way that others see and recognize. Create an atmosphere where everyone understands and places high value on positive reinforcement. Become a model of positive reinforcement and be sure to provide deserved praise.

Too often leaders become distracted with the immediate crisis and dive right into meetings about the urgent problems of the day. This is often complicated by an imperfect understanding of the operations or products in the merging group. They forget that every day there will be a new problem and that the culture is what allows for a resolution to these issues. Spending a few minutes at the start of each meeting reflecting on what is going right makes sure everyone is in top shape with a winning attitude and gives the group the ability to tackle any problem.

The key is to create a reinforcing culture at all levels. It isn't enough for just the boss or a few supervisors to reinforce good culture. Teach everyone to do it. As the culture develops and integrates, you'll see it spreading to other parts of the organization. People will begin to notice that the combined area is much more positive and productive than before.

Positive reinforcement builds confidence. As Jack Stack wrote in *The Great Game of Business* (2013, 76), "One of a manager's main responsibilities is to build confidence in the organization. To do that, you have to accentuate the positive. If you accentuate the negative, it eats away at the organization. It becomes a demotivator." A reinforcing culture transforms an organization from looking for a "what's wrong" mindset to focusing on "what's right." The positive energy benefits everyone as the culture is significantly enhanced. In addition, the quality and quantity of work increases dramatically because you have harnessed energy previously lost in bickering and put it to work toward the combined vision. What an uplifting way to increase productivity! Instead of beating on people and constantly dwelling on the negative, you'll be generating good feelings and loyalty while you drive productivity.

Don't get discouraged if you make a mistake. Sometimes you will. Reinforcement is an area of significant peril, but its power is immense. Continually monitor your success level with positive reinforcement. Talk about it openly and work to improve the culture. Consider every mistake a learning event for everyone, especially yourself. Let your positive reinforcement be joyous and spontaneous. Let people help you make it special. This is the most powerful elixir available to a leader. Don't shy away from it because it's difficult or you've made mistakes in the past.

Integrate New Methods Into the Culture

Make sure you document procedures in a user-friendly way. Avoid long complex manuals that nobody has the time to read. Have a checklist for new employees and make sure they understand the culture. Reinforce consistent behaviors. A great deal of cross training needs to be done before full integration can occur. If you have a new process that uses a different software package, you have to make sure people are trained and rewarded when they use the new system instead of going back to old solutions.

Demonstrate a Constant Purpose

Effective change programs require a constant purpose. Keep focused on the main goals and avoid the training programs that create unnecessary diversions. Expect setbacks as part of the process and change initiatives when things get rough. Instead, refer to the activities as working on culture. For example, an organization may be working on an effort to increase participation or reduce exclusivity. In the middle of that effort it would be confusing to start a major initiative to reduce waste.

Understand the Psychology of Change

If you think of change as a system with its own inner process, you can help people through the process more quickly. Recognize there will be confusion or anger and use that energy to propel the process forward rather than slow it down.

The grief counseling model helps groups move through the phases of change efficiently. When humans experience grief due to an unexpected situation, they become incapable of performing in a normal way. They usually can eat something to stay alive. They may be able to sleep a little if they get tired enough, but they are not a fully functioning human being.

Figure 16.1: Grief Counseling Model

A grief counselor can be very effective at allowing the person to return to full function much sooner than would be possible on her own. Basically the grief counselor walks the grieving person through a well-defined process that leads to recovery. It works because there is a road-map of emotional reactions that most people experience when facing change. The model has four major parts with several typical symptoms in each part.

Anticipation

In the anticipation phase, people become aware of new opportunities or threats. They may see the need to change coming in the future. A typical comment made in the anticipating phase is that "the writing is on the wall." Denial is common during the anticipating phase. People just can't believe this is happening. When facing reorganization, antici-pation most correlates to the time when rumors start through the time of the announcement.

Ending

The next phase is the ending phase. Fear of loss is the most common reaction in this phase. We see that we need to move out of our comfort zone into an area that is scary. In the ending phase we feel the sadness and depression for the loss. This phase is often compared to a death because it is the end of what was there before and people need to adjust to it. The announcement introduces irrevocable change and people are uncertain about the future as they contemplate what will happen next.

Transition

The transition phase, where most of the action occurs, is usually the longest phase of the process. In transition, rumors and speculation take over. People begin to bargain for a better deal. Denial is also common in the transition phase, and there is a great deal of chaos within the organization. In the transition phase, anger and hostility are common occurrences. People may choose sides and form into cliques. During the transition phase leadership is essential to help lead people through these emotional times and avoid a significant loss of trust.

Beginning

Finally we reach the beginning phase where acceptance occurs. We select the path forward and begin to communicate that new path. We enroll the team in the new methods, and we start to rebuild enthusiasm.

Summary

I like to use this grief counseling model when coaching teams through difficult change processes like a merger. It works because people can see a logical progression and they realize that if they are angry today that is just part of the process. It will pass as they move on to the next phase. The ability to see change as a sequence of events that are controllable and manageable helps people move through the change process much more rapidly.

All large changes are challenging for people, so using the grief counseling model is a great tool for leaders. It can allow a transition that might have taken a year to fully assimilate, to be done in a couple months. That time saving is incredibly important because it shortens the chaos period when the customer may be negatively impacted.

Surviving and thriving during a time of great change requires organizations to have a solid set of shared values and make sure they abide by them. Many organizations have good values, but fail to live by them on a daily basis.

Food for Thought

1. Name a large change program in your organization that took too long. What techniques in this chapter would have been most helpful?

2. What is the best method for dealing with people who cannot get on board with a change?

3. Too many changes in rapid succession can really confuse people. What is your estimate of the required time between change initiatives to allow people time to assimilate before launching into another one?

17

Focus on the Big Picture

*"You can't depend on your eyes when your
imagination is out of focus."*

Mark Twain

In this chapter you will learn:

- Anticipate a difficult period of more than a year when doing a major reorganization.
- Put a plan in place to keep the core business going during the integration.
- Employ the six antidotes as much as possible.
- Do not cut staff too early.

During the run up to a major change initiative, the details of the deal become so overwhelming that people in the organization can become distracted. After the announcement, conditions become even more confusing and often the organizations fail to do what is required to sustain the business while the new processes are being put in place.

This chapter is about the dangers of being distracted. In the corporate situation, we have the leaders of an organization fully occupied with trying to optimize a business. It is common to have top-level people regularly working as much as 80 hours a week. Picture two independent groups with both sets of managers under the same extreme pressure and all of a sudden overlay a huge project that takes their attention away from their main function for the majority of time every day for eight months.

It is not hard to see how the business fundamentals suffer while the process is playing out up to the announcement. All kinds of things need to be delegated to people who may not be as adept at handling them. They will do the best they can, but some issues are going to slip through the cracks. These problems tend to surface at the worst possible time because each company is trying to maximize every aspect of the business for valuation purposes during due diligence.

For example, accounts receivable is an area that sometimes requires a lot of attention. With somewhat lower attention to the details of collections, accounts receivable may climb to an abnormally high level just as the financial scrutiny is going on. The same phenomenon occurs in every area of the business.

Sales and customer service are not forgotten, but they will receive lower involvement from managers during the negotiation process, which impacts the top line income just when income needs to be as robust as possible. Every facet of the business in both companies is being impacted to some degree during the pre-announcement phases of reorganization. Performance appraisals and training are the first to go.

Following the announcement, things actually get worse in terms of distractions. Before the announcement, at least the lower level staff is operating normally. They may be a bit distracted because of the rumors, but their world has not changed that much. After the announcement, not only is management distracted trying to figure out how to integrate two businesses into one, but every single person in both organizations is feeling sidetracked.

The staffs of both organizations realize jobs will be cut to reduce redundant staff. New roles are not often clear at the beginning, so people do their best under uncertain conditions. Meanwhile, the customers are not interested in reasons or excuses; they just want their product or service on time, with perfect quality, at the expected price.

Most reorganization efforts take more than a year to sort out, but that is a long time for two organizations to be in limbo. Even a few days of chaos are enough to create the loss of business performance. What then are the antidotes for the distraction problem?

Higher Empowerment

Involve employees in figuring out the future processes to move beyond the grieving process and get people engaged in the new configuration.

Giving more staff greater power to figure out the rules will help because:

- They are the closest to the work, so they have the best ideas on how to do things better.
- They will become engaged in helping create the future rather than longing for the past.
- They will be less inclined to look for employment elsewhere.
- They will usually step up to higher responsibility if given the chance.
- The leaders will have more time to focus on the strategy and not get involved in so many details.

Discipline

Every function in the organization needs to be clearly defined so that maximum flexibility is possible. Cross training is one technique to ensure there is enough bench strength to operate more like a MASH unit than a municipal hospital for extended periods.

Ken Blanchard likes to tell a story about when he went into a DMV to renew his license and was blown away with the responsive organization. He was in and out, including a picture, in nine minutes. He asked what the difference was and it turned out to be the new leader. Ken asked him what his job was and the leader said, "My job is to reorganize the department on a moment to moment basis depending on citizen need." You can see his cartoon video "It's Always the Leader" on YouTube. The video emphasizes the benefits of cross training workers and having a flexible work flow based on current needs.

A different kind of discipline is for leaders to resist the temptation to become consumed with making the deal. Leaders need to compartmentalize their time by devoting sufficient time to their former responsibilities to keep the ship afloat, while the change effort takes a back seat to satisfying customers or working with delinquent suppliers when necessary. Since the reorganization effort is titillating and forward thinking, it takes great discipline to set it aside when required. Masterful management of your calendar can help and wringing out any time spent on nonessential tasks is mandatory.

Smart Deployment

Set up a few people who will handle the heavy lifting for the change effort while the remainder of the staff keeps the business running. People will usually rise to a challenge, provided they can see a better future as a payoff. If the vision of why everyone needs to work so much harder is clouded, then people will be asking "What's in it for me" when they are called upon to stretch.

Outsource Some Functions

Normally any kind of reorganization will have a set of outside advisors or consultants to help with the details. This is because most managers are not trained on the nitty-gritty rules and procedures for accomplishing a business consolidation. For example, the accounting firm that helped with the due diligence phase may be helpful during the integration at working with the staff to set up the new combined accounting procedures.

Manage Staffing Levels Wisely

Most organizations like to run lean in standard business conditions. They can flex up or down a bit by asking people to stretch or work overtime. Many managers listen to the complaints about workload to help them determine when they need to hire more people or cut back. If they hear no complaining, then they think they have too much staff. If there is a reasonable amount of griping about the workload, they think it is just about right. If people are in a state of revolt, then they need to add some resources. If there will be an extended period where staff is going to be insanely tight while the deal is struck and the transition occurs, it would not be wise to sail into that period with all of your employees already overloaded.

After the big announcement, it is tempting to start cutting people because there will be some obvious functional redundancy. Be careful about cashing in redundant staff too early in the process. You may need to go a little more slowly than planned because people are not going to be working at peak productivity due to confusion and demoralization. This is one area where the initial ROI calculation sends managers down the wrong path. The initial look showed that we could reduce the staff level by 25 percent and be able to operate after a merger. Well, that may be the case once things have settled, but if you accomplish your calculated lower staff level in the second week after the announcement, you may be in for a rude awakening by week three.

Have a Detailed Plan

A promise without a plan will get you fired. A plan helps people meet their goals by understanding the assumptions, risks, and steps to the desired outcome. The more detailed the plan is, the greater the possibility of getting through it with grace. Consultants experienced with transitions have the background to help managers anticipate issues and put plans in place to address them ahead of time. Working ahead of problems as much as possible results in less chaos and improves morale. Being able to explain plans and functions in detail at the time of the announcement is a credibility boosting situation for the managers.

Too often we see managers say, "Well, we are going to merge with Acorn Tool this month. We have not figured out who is going to stay and who is going to leave. In fact, we do not even know how many people we need yet. In the meantime, do the best you can to get along and perform up to your usual excellence." This kind of announcement leads to instant panic.

The process leading up to an integration or a major business reorganization is usually a harrowing experience for any organization. It is common to have executives halfway through the ordeal wish they had never thought of the plan. Too late. You cannot go back; you can only go forward. The best advice is to expect a rough trip and to not overstate what is possible when you set the objectives. Massive change is hard work and it needs proper staffing levels.

Food for Thought

1. Think about a reorganization effort that went really well. Describe the planning that was done.

2. Describe the kind of chaos that occurs when most people do not know their future or what they are supposed to be doing on the job tomorrow. What steps need to be taken first to help reduce the problems?

3. Why is it that most estimated timelines for full integration are way too optimistic?

18

Clone Yourself

*"Cloning, wow. Who would have thought? There should be
a list of people who can and cannot clone themselves."*

Ted Danson

In this chapter you will learn:

- Asking people to double up with two functions is tempting, but dangerous.
- It is important to be transparent with the plan as soon as you legally can.
- Never tell an employee "you are lucky to have a job."
- Downsizing is never easy.

There is a curious phenomenon where sometimes people are asked to keep up their old workload (which was a full time job) and simultaneously absorb the full responsibilities of a second person who was let go following a merger. This doesn't make sense.

This practice is common and almost always disastrous. The reason is that the additional job responsibilities are typically dumped on the unprepared employee who has had no opportunity to train with the prior employee. The sheer workload of double job responsibilities often cripples motivation, so the frustrated employee does a poor job on both functions. The irony is that this employee was formerly viewed as one of the best in the organization (and survived the cut), but within a few months, this same superstar is viewed as—and often feels like—a loser. This result is almost inevitable and disastrous for the employee, the organization, and the customers.

How does this happen? Let's go back to the beginning. Rumors start as a result of all the secret meetings. Layoffs are expected, because one primary result of a merger is to consolidate staff positions. People are aware of this and hope they will be one of the survivors. However, some people are smart enough to hope they do not survive.

The executives announce the merger, but it is really not a shock to the people in the organization. They are just glad to have the news out in the open. Being held in the dark is a most uncomfortable feeling and the lack of transparency has a negative impact on the organization. In fact, this lack turns out to be far more deadly for the organization than anyone realizes at this point.

The day for lay-offs finally arrives. The boss calls people in one by one to tell them the bad news. Guards walk them back to their area to get their belongings and then escort them out the gate. A quick handshake and the surrender of the employee pass is all it takes to complete the deal. Oh sure, there is the promise of support from HR: "Go to a place off company property over the next week and we will help you network in the community for another job." A packet arrives in the mail to sign up for COBRA insurance to tide over the family.

As it turns out, everyone is impacted, but in different ways. Here is a typical story about what happens to those who stay.

Bill is a great service technician who thinks he has not been affected. Bill's boss, Gloria, calls him into her office and explains that Bill still has a job, but he is being asked to perform his old function plus cover for Ashley, who was let go earlier that day. Bill becomes upset and says, "How am I going to do that? I barely keep up with the load as it is! Right now I have three customers who are annoyed because it has taken me over a week to get their computers repaired. You want me to do Ashley's work too? I do not even know anything about the modules she has been repairing! This is ridiculous!"

Gloria reminds Bill that he is "lucky to have a job at all," but Bill is already starting to doubt that. It is a typical response from clueless managers to tell an over-burdened employee that he is lucky to have a job. We are about to see what "lucky" really means. In the long term, it is the manager who is the unlucky one.

Bill does the best he can, but he has real problems doing Ashley's job for three reasons: he is overloaded, he does not know Ashley's customers, and he has not been trained to repair the modules that Ashley handled. He keeps struggling trying to keep up and cover his mistakes using instructions in the manual. After a couple weeks, he goes in to see Gloria and reiterates that the double assignment is not going to work. This time Gloria is as clueless as she was at first. She tells Bill, "There is nothing I can do to reverse this and Ashley is long gone. Just suck it up and get things done the best you can." Bill shrugs and says "Thanks a lot."

Over the next two weeks, Bill tries to outflank the problem by working crazy hours. He is a morning person, so he skips his exercise time to get into work before 5 a.m. That is a quiet time where he can concentrate on learning how to repair the modules that were formerly Ashley's responsibility. He feels that he is gaining knowledge, but he cannot deal with the load of two people's work. He is falling behind, even though he works until 8 p.m. most evenings, which forces him to miss his daughter's soccer games. Bill's wife is legitimately worried about his health and starts nagging him to get a physical, but he has no time to go see a doctor. Finally, he does take a couple hours and go in for some tests. His doctor is astounded at the slide in his physical condition and gives Bill some bad news.

Meanwhile, back at the office, Gloria's boss has been getting pounded by customers demanding their equipment be returned so they can take it somewhere else to get repaired. They are losing money because the service organization is not getting the job done. The big boss runs into Gloria's office and yells at her that these complaints have to stop or she will be fired. Gloria runs down the hall to Bill's workstation. She says, "Bill, you have been one of our best technicians, yet you are letting us down and customers want their computers back immediately. We cannot afford to have customers defecting!"

Bill takes a deep breath and calmly says, "You are right Gloria, we cannot afford to let the customers down. Also, I cannot afford to work here for you anymore. I am giving you my two-week notice as of now. My wife and family tell me I am a basket case, and my doctor says I am heading for a stroke."

Now the organization is really going to suffer because Bill has little impetus to do a good job for the remaining two weeks and nobody else knows how to do Bill's or Ashley's work. Gloria will soon lose her job as well, but it is the organization that will suffer the most.

Looking back at the root cause of the whole mess, the lack of transparency looms the largest. It is more important for employees to understand the reason for a decision than the decision itself. To see why, let's replay the scenario in a way that the staff could have been reduced without the disastrous results.

First, Gloria would have been allowed to tell people that "sometime during the next quarter we will need to downsize and I will be asking people to do some cross training starting next week. I will let the impacted people know many weeks before termination so they can help train those who will inherit their work. They will also be given some personal time to look for a job while they still are employed. It is much easier to find a job when you have a job."

Next, Gloria would inform Ashley that she will likely be impacted and ask her to train Bill on her responsibilities. Gloria would immediately talk with Bill explaining the plan to shift much of Ashley's workload over to him and begin a process of working through all of Bill's responsibilities to remove some of the administrative or other burdens to make it possible for him to accommodate the increased load. For example, suppose Bill spent about six hours a week planning and conducting the Quality Meeting. This work could actually be accomplished by distributing the Weekly Quality Summary and eliminate the need for the meeting unless there was a major problem. This would reduce Bills workload by six hours a week.

In the discussion with Bill, Gloria stresses that he is a highly valued employee being called on to stretch his influence with the customer base. A reduction in other activities will provide some relief in order to allow him more time to make repairs. Bill will also receive a modest bump in pay as a result of the increased responsibility.

I grant that this second scenario is far from easy or painless for all parties, but the consequences are far less debilitating for the business. By treating all employees well from the start and leveling with them, many of the problems in the first scenario can be prevented. The most significant reason for the difference between the two cases is that the top boss or HR professional allowed the local manager to operate with transparency before the layoffs.

In the next chapter we look at one specific function that is critical to the entire effort but that often gets overlooked. It is easy to disregard the plight of the frontline supervisor in reorganization efforts and that is a huge pitfall.

Food for Thought

1. Think of some best practices in downsizing. The process is difficult, but if you show you care you will do a better job.

2. In the scenario in this chapter, what could have Gloria done to improve her chances of survival?

3. How can you ensure there is adequate time to train a replacement before someone leaves?

19

Support Frontline Supervision

"Any supervisor worth his salt would rather deal with people who attempt too much than with those who try too little."

Lee Iacocca

In this chapter you will learn to:

- Focus energy on the frontline supervisor position.
- Assess who is truly onboard and who may resist the change.
- Train the supervisors on better leadership as a combined group.
- Adopt possible troublemakers and save the ones you can. Get rid of the others.

This chapter shines a light on the difficult but crucial role of the frontline supervisor in making the reorganization work. There are some unique issues that make supervisors particularly vulnerable but at the same time extremely valuable. Get this part wrong and you will severely hamper the reorganization; get it right and you will be halfway to success.

The common thread with frontline supervisors is that these people operate at the critical and delicate junction between management layers and workers on the frontline. Depending on the type of work being done, supervisors come from a variety of backgrounds. The typical history is that the supervisor was once an individual contributor who did very well on the job over a long period of time. Through dedication and deep content knowledge, this person sparkled relative to her counterparts. When an opportunity arose, this individual was tapped to become a supervisor.

Another common trait of supervisors is that they are often put on the job with little training. They already have deep process knowledge and have shown a natural tendency toward informal leadership, so they are given the responsibility. Often they receive no training at first and later it is forgotten because the person does just fine from the start. There is, however, a lurking weakness that surfaces during any kind of reorganization.

The attitudes of supervisors during a merger or acquisition are critical influences to how the employees react to the change. More than any other relationship in the organization, trust is maintained or lost by the workers' relationship with their direct supervisor. If supervisors model a cooperative and adventurous spirit and keep looking for the good, it can help people see that positive outcomes are possible. If the supervisors are rolling their eyes and visibly displaying their own fears, then that attitude is going to be picked up and amplified by the people who work for them. It is impossible to act out positive behaviors if they are not deeply implanted, because people are reading body language at every interaction and they will pick up the true attitude of the supervisor quickly.

In reorganizations, the operational processes are subject to combinations or modifications in order to accommodate the changing nature of the business. Often the new entity will be a combination of companies with completely different cultures, perhaps even different languages. This new dynamic could be threatening to supervisors, since their license to lead is often their familiarity with the work rather than deep leadership skills. Changing their work means their platform to lead has been weakened. Couple that with the inevitable push to reduce supervisory headcount and you have an opportunity for some terrified people in these roles. You absolutely cannot afford to have any weakness showing through to the workers during the process and the supervisor is the critical link to demonstrate the management point of view. This can be a huge problem in a transition. Thankfully there are approaches to deal with the issue.

Training

The antidote here is training and the cost for the training program should be included in the original financial analysis. Frontline leaders need more skills during a transition. They also will require some cultural training if the combined organization involves groups from other cultures. The training should begin as early as possible and contain supervisors from both groups so that early team bonding can occur. Getting to know the frontline leaders in the other half of the organization will pay huge dividends as the process unfolds. For one thing, these supervisors will be more easily interchanged later on. Also, having personal relationships with other supervisors enables more sharing of resources. This integrated training is a major way to prevent the "us versus them" thinking that hobbles so many reorganizations.

Coaching

Another suggestion is to develop a "coaching corner" for all supervisors. This is a mechanism for management to work face-to-face with supervisors during the planning and execution phases. It is important to have all supervisors emotionally engaged and pulling in the direction you wish to go. If they favor a different path, they will take the spirit of the masses in the wrong direction every time and you will not get them back easily. Special briefings and team activities for supervisors will keep them actively supporting the effort because they are helping to design it. Remember the old adage, "Change done to me is scary, but change done by me is energizing."

Convert or Remove Naysayers

Finally, it is vital to cull out any supervisors who would sabotage the effort, even unwittingly. It is not hard to determine who might undermine the effort. Some supervisors will not agree with the change. Try to convert those who would push against the change. Many times, through careful attention by management, an individual can be turned around. I call this process "adopting a supervisor."

Basically, the manager gets very close to the supervisor through a series of informal conversations to figure out what makes the person tick. It takes time to do this, but the payoff is very high. The advantage is that after a while you get to identify which reluctant supervisors are worth trying to save. Focus your efforts on them and develop a plan to move the others out of leadership positions. This action can, and should, be done routinely, but it becomes an essential ingredient during reorganization. You cannot afford to have a supervisor who is not completely on board with the effort. He will poison the people who work for him.

The most wonderful part of this coaching process is that you have the opportunity to turn certain powerful negative forces in the organization into powerful allies. Keep in mind that the supervisor was originally selected based on her ability to be an informal leader. Turning a negative person into a positive force is a huge swing in the right direction. If you can simultaneously remove the sour individual who will never change, that is also a blessing.

Adopting a supervisor may seem like a very time-consuming effort. The change is not going to occur in a week, but the daily time investment is not great. What it takes is resolve and persistence to work with those you want to convert. Select the people who are worthy of your limited time and invest in them.

Food for Thought

1. What tools would you use to determine a supervisor's true attitude toward a change?

2. What percentage of supervisors in your organization do you think can be turned around through careful attention and coaching over an extended period?

3. How would you go about removing supervisors who you think will never get on board?

20

Trust and Motivation

"The best morale exists when you never hear the word mentioned. When you hear a lot of talk about it, it's usually lousy."

Dwight D. Eisenhower

In this chapter you will learn:

- A great culture provides motivation. Focus on the culture and you will see higher morale and motivation as a result.

- There are nine methods to build a stronger culture.

- It does not take years to establish a new culture. With the proper leadership in place, the time to make a huge improvement is weeks rather than years.

As the integration starts, the ability to grow trust becomes the most important enabler of success. It is particularly challenging because people are anxious about their future. They also have a new cast of characters to deal with who are mostly unknown to them. Trust will be difficult to kindle and grow under these circumstances.

For leaders, it is important to focus on building a culture of trust for the future. If this is done well, morale and motivation will be enhanced. Morale and motivation are not objectives; they are the outcomes of a corporate culture. If leaders spend their time and energy trying to improve the environment and increase trust, then higher morale and motivation will happen naturally.

I have seen a group of people at work with such low motivation there seemed to be no way to get any work done. If a manager dared try to speak to a group of employees, they would heckle or just not pay attention. Nothing the leader said or did had much impact on the employees, so in desperation, the manager would use threats. This would elicit a halfhearted groan and some compliance for a time, but the quality of work would suffer and the gains were only temporary. Imagine a merger situation where both groups are equally grumpy. It takes a special kind of leader to come in to that situation and quickly build the right kind of culture, but I have seen it done in just a few months.

How was that leader able to accomplish a turnaround in just six months amid the chaos of a merger? The leader focused on changing the underlying culture to one of high trust rather than just demanding improvement. The motivation and morale improved as a result of the improved culture rather than because they were the objective.

Let's look at some specific steps this manager took that turned things around quickly.

Build Trust

She immediately let people know she was not there to play games with them. She told them that making improvements in their work life was foremost in her mind. She let people know it was safe to come to her with any issue and know they would not be insulted or punished. She told people the truth about what was happening with staffing decisions and made herself available for anyone who wanted to vent.

Improve Teamwork

She invested in some off-site teamwork training for the entire group. These workshops made a big difference in breaking down barriers between the groups and teaching people how to get along better in normal organizational life.

Empower Others

She made sure the expectations of all workers were known to them but did not micromanage the process. She let people figure out how to accomplish tasks and got rid of several arcane and restrictive rules that were holding people back from giving their maximum discretionary effort. Every time she would do away with a stupid rule, they would have a little celebration. She assigned special roles to key people on the team to help knit the organizations together and stood behind them even if they made some mistakes along the way. The manager also supported people when they had personal needs, and made sure the organization received the funding necessary to buy better equipment and tools.

Remove People When Needed

She worked to create a set of shared values for the combined department and got rid of people who were unable to follow them. This showed that the values were more than a plaque on the wall. Whenever a bad actor was terminated, there was an immediate sense of relief, because people no longer had to work around his or her antics.

Reinforce Progress

The atmosphere became lighter and more fun for the workers as they started to feel more successful and really enjoyed the creative reinforcement activities set up by their leader. She let the workers plan their own celebrations, within reasonable guidelines, and participated in the activities herself. She made sure that any celebrations were for the combined group and did not tolerate parochial thinking between the two prior organizations.

Promote Good Work

The manager held a series of meetings with higher management to showcase the progress in an improved culture. The workers were involved in planning and conducting these meetings, so they got the benefit of praise directly from top management. To the extent possible the manager let people in the groups be a part of the staffing discussions. This helped a lot.

Set Tough Goals

The manager did not set weak or easy goals. Instead, she set aggressive stretch goals and explained her faith that the team could achieve them. At first, people seemed worried about the enormity of her challenges, but that soon gave way to elation as milestones were reached.

Be Firm But Fair

The manager was consistent in her application of discipline. People respected her for not playing favorites and for making some tough choices that were right in the long run. Her strength was evident in her decisions every day, so people grew in their respect for her. She did not favor one group over the other and made sure there was no perception of a bias. She put a lot of effort into being fair to both groups.

Summary

This manager turned a near-hopeless workforce of two former separate groups into a team of highly motivated individuals in six months. Morale was incredibly high. Even though improving morale was not the objective, it was an outcome of her actions to improve the culture.

If you want to be an elite leader, even in a time of organizational change, work on the culture of your organization. Develop trust and treat people the right way and you will see a remarkable transformation in an amazingly short period of time.

Food for Thought

1. Why does having a program to improve motivation usually fail to produce the desired result?

2. How would you advise a new manager who is taking over a tough situation with jaded employees?

21

Accountability

*"When it comes to privacy and accountability,
people always demand the former for themselves
and the latter for everyone else."*

David Brin

In this chapter you will learn:

- Holding people accountable is normally a negative statement.
- Work to make accountability more balanced.

Accountability is the central issue for making culture changes work. Holding people accountable seems to be a mantra for managers. During a reorganization or merger, accountability takes on added significance. People are on edge and not necessarily thinking clearly. This can lead to quality or safety errors. Many people will be assuming new roles without much time for cross training. Just knowing the people within the team will be a challenge because people will be moving around. All performance metrics can take a hit for these reasons, yet top management is still expecting near-perfect levels of performance and holding people accountable for that.

For example, in a transition, a supervisor may be held accountable for making sure his employees are trained on jobs from the other side of the organization. Not doing enough training could pose a real danger during the integration. The supervisor is torn between trying to get the training done and producing high quality products at the expected level.

Most managers use the words "hold them accountable." This directive almost always means that someone has fallen short of expectations and the manager needs to point out that lapse and have a discussion about improving performance.

I have developed a strategy for holding people accountable in ways that enable trust. Imagine how the world would be different if we transformed accountability from a negative concept to a positive one. The manager would reflect on the many ways an individual is doing well and measuring up to, or exceeding, expectations. In the supervisor example above, things may not be perfect amid the chaos, but if she has a solid plan and is making steady progress, management can offer praise and support.

For most people, being held accountable would become a positive experience that would encourage more of those actions rather than instill fear. Sure, there would be times when a person did not measure up to expectations, so the discussion would point out that the intentions of the individual did not produce the expected result in this instance. Some coaching may be needed, but most of the accountability discussions would be supportive and lead to higher productivity.

Let's say that in an acquisition, a quality manager is supposed to make sure all the procedures are up-to-date and published, so the quality process of his company can be rationalized with the process of the firm to be acquired. The manager assembles the documentation and hands over the materials on time. In the review, they find that a couple processes refer to a device that is no longer produced by the organization. Those sections should have been deleted, but were not. The oversight is acknowledged and corrected, but the bulk of accountability is for the job that was done well, with only slight mention of the minor issue.

The logic here is that most people come to work on most days with the intention of doing things right. Very few people actually try to mess up at work. If you find any who do, get rid of them as fast as you can. So, if most people are doing the right things most of the time, we could have numerous discussions about their successes.

Operating in the confusion and extra demands of a merger or reorganization requires special fortitude and this is where the concept of holding people accountable for success as well as mistakes can provide great leverage in building trust. When an occasional lapse does happen, negative feedback would be the exception rather than the rule. That difference alone would change the equation greatly. If 95 percent of the feedback is supportive comments and only 5 percent is potential improvements, the working environment would be a much better place for most employees.

Unfortunately, most organizations obsess about holding people accountable, so the feedback employees hear from managers and supervisors is 95 percent negative and only 5 percent supportive. This is especially true in the challenging times of integration. After a while, the culture gets beaten down, and the need for more corrective and punitive discussions becomes more frequent. The common phrase uttered by thousands of workers over the decades is "the only time I ever hear from my boss is when I screw up." That condition undermines trust at any point in the process.

The advice here is quite simple and logical. Simply work to make accountability a balanced phenomenon in proportion to the actual performance of the people involved. That will improve the integrated culture and enable trust.

Food for Thought

1. How would the environment in your workplace change if feedback discussions were not always negative? Would the resulting culture have higher trust?

2. Think about how your current organization holds people accountable. Is it helpful or hurtful? How could it be improved?

Part V:

The Games People Play

This part looks at several roles played by people during an integration. We will take a look at some of the problem personalities that appear when reorganization occurs. To understand the tapestry of actions and emotions brought about by several of these characters operating at the same time, we need to look at the entire melting pot. There are numerous other types of people also impacting the process, but in my experience, the ones mentioned in this part seem to cause the most problems. For each case, I will describe what the behavior is, why it generally occurs, the harm it can cause, and some antidotes or coping mechanisms.

22

Narcissistic Bosses

"But by most measures, narcissism is one of the worst [personality disorders], if only because the narcissists themselves are so clueless."

Jeffrey Kluger

In this chapter you will learn:

- Narcissist leaders are common, and there are varying degrees of the problem.
- Leaders with these tendencies will cause problems during a change effort.
- There are some ways to chip away at the problem, but they are a lot of work and sometimes backfire.
- The real cure is to build higher trust through reinforcing candor. That will usually work, but it is difficult to get the leader to try because of ego.

In any merger or acquisition, the characteristics of the top leaders in both organizations heavily impact the resulting merged culture. The sad truth is that in many mergers, one or both of the top players are narcissists to some degree. In psychiatry, narcissism is a personality disorder characterized by a patient's overestimation of his or her own appearance and abilities, along with an excessive need for admiration.

I believe most people suffer from some degree of this disorder, but in most cases the symptoms are mild and under control. In business, the higher you go in an organization the greater the chances you will run into a hard case of narcissism. The reason is pretty obvious. A person who rises to the top of an organization has obviously gone through a lot. She may have gotten there by luck, being in the right place at the right time, great skills, nepotism, or it could even have been a mistake, but however it happened, she has arrived at the pinnacle where people have to listen to her opinion and accept it most of the time. She suffers from "I am right" syndrome. It is a rare leader that does not get a somewhat inflated view of her skills and importance while enjoying the perks of the executive suite. Occasionally you do find a humble leader running an organization, and usually these leaders are the most effective, as pointed out by Jim Collins in *Good to Great*. I am not implying that all CEOs are narcissists, but the odds of having two senior executives negotiating for a reorganization deal where neither of them exhibits any tendency toward narcissism are very low.

Let's first examine the case where one CEO has a serious case of narcissism but the other is a humble leader with no tendency toward it at all. The negotiation will lean heavily in favor of the more aggressive CEO, but the more unassuming leader may gain some advantage at times by being passive aggressive or just plain stubborn. It is likely that the two individuals are not going to trust each other much, so every decision will be a hard won.

They are going to drive each other crazy, but the narcissist leader will likely enjoy the sport. After the announcement, the narcissist will want to run the show in terms of decisions, so it is likely that he will be on top, even if the deal is advertised as a merger of equals. If the humble leader can tolerate being second in command after being the big deal in his own organization, then the two may be able to coexist reasonably well into the integration phase. If not, then the likely scenario is that a gracious exit for the humble leader will be built into the deal even before the announcement.

In many reorganization efforts, you have both CEOs actively involved with all of their warts and egoisms. It is common to have two narcissists at the negotiating table for a merger. They may not be doing all of the actual negotiations, but they are pulling the strings on everything that goes on. It becomes a battle of wits—although in reality both of the CEOs may be rather witless—each leader can only perceive the tendency in the other individual, not himself.

If the winner is not crowned at the negotiating phase, then the battle will rage on during the integration of the teams. Both CEOs will pretend to get along, but underneath, each will be trying to undermine the other. The CEOs are not modeling the behaviors they are requesting the other people to follow, which leads to a very weak integration and a lot of game playing on the part of both teams. The reorganization will be off to a terrible start making the probability of failure very high.

The entire process, from idea to fully integrated steady-state environment, will require people to work around the problems created at the top. Moreover, if the two top leaders preach love, respect, and brotherhood while secretly plotting the ouster of their rival, it will model enmity that will be amplified throughout the combined organization.

Tips for Dealing With a Narcissistic Boss

Is the situation hopeless? What methods can we use to get through to a narcissistic boss? It is a delicate balance that involves helping an ego-driven leader recognize when he or she is actually operating against the stated vision. There are three tips that may be helpful in some cases, but sometimes the best you can hope for is to mitigate some of the symptoms.

Ask Questions

One way for employees to help the CEO be more amenable to their ideas lies in asking questions rather than making statements. Using the Socratic Method of asking open-ended questions in a carefully orchestrated sequence, it is sometimes possible to have the desired course of action offered first by the leader. He may be unaware that his opinion has been shaped or crafted by the sequence of questions he was asked. Once the approach has been uttered by the leader as his idea, people can praise him for being so brilliant, and then implement "his plan," which is what the employee wanted to do in the first place. If instead of asking questions, they had approached him with a statement or a proposal to do the exact same thing, he might have rejected the plan.

This tip does not attempt to change the narcissistic tendencies of the leader, but actually uses the disorder to navigate around the problem. The method can be helpful to obtain backing for a specific course of action, but it should be used sparingly lest the ploy be detected by the leader. If the CEO starts to detect manipulation, then all bets are off, and he won't be happy.

Try Leadership Development

A second method is to get buy-in for some leadership development work for the entire group. The reason this method can work is that no situation is perfect and narcissist leaders rarely see themselves as the source of the problem. They tend to blame their employees for the issues that they themselves created. In this case, it may be possible to get the afflicted leader to agree to some kind of development activity for all leaders including herself. A benign type of improvement forum is a weekly lunch-and-learn development session with volunteers from the senior staff, which includes the CEO in the discussions. The group votes on a leadership book to read and study, then the group meets to discuss the techniques or theories they have been learning.

Over time, the group can bring up some of the behaviors of the senior leader that are not helping the cause. Because the program is billed and sold as a development activity for all leaders, it reduces the feeling that people are targeting the CEO. He may eventually see himself more accurately. This group coaching is best facilitated by an outside person to keep the discussions from taking a negative tone.

Improve Emotional Intelligence

A third approach is to work on the emotional intelligence of the CEO. The problem with a narcissist leader is that she has a blind spot relative to how she is affecting other people. That symptom is a classic indicator of low emotional intelligence. Some specific coaching for the leader might be beneficial for opening her eyes to how her behaviors are at least partially to blame for the problems in the organization.

It is hard to convince a narcissist leader that she should get some emotional intelligence coaching because she cannot see herself as the source of the problem. A coach would work on softening this denial first. It is hard work for the consultant because as soon as the coach hints that the CEO's worst enemy is herself, the consultant may be rejected by the leader.

Summary

These tips for dealing with a narcissist leader are applicable to an organization whether or not they are in a reorganization effort. But when a transition is in play, there are often two leaders involved with each one having the problem to some degree. It gets very complicated. No amount of classic teambuilding activities will be very helpful. In fact, efforts to get people to work well together may backfire if the two CEOs are subtly working at odds with each other. People can see the root cause of the acrimony, but they cannot say or do anything about it. The only way out of the mess is to find a mirror so both CEOs can see their part in creating the issues.

The mirror I am describing is trust. Without high trust between the leaders at various levels in both groups, people are simply playing head games with each other. Outsiders can see this kind of behavior easily and insiders realize it is going on but can't figure out how to break the cycle. What it takes is a different approach that stops the game playing. I call that approach "reinforcing candor."

If the CEOs start praising employees when they bring up apparent inconsistencies between what the leader is saying and doing, the equation will change rapidly. Few leaders have the courage to do this, simply because of their egos. Those who can understand the wisdom of this approach, and begin to do more of it, will start to build higher trust. Very quickly the games will stop and a better environment will begin to emerge. In that environment, people will feel liberated to share when the boss is acting against the objectives, and they know they will not get clobbered when they do it. Now the organization can move out of the dysfunctional mess and begin to build a future on a firm foundation of trust.

Food for Thought

1. It is pivotal to reduce or eliminate the problems created at the top. What other suggestions can you think of to help the CEO see himself more accurately as part of the problem?

2. In what ways can you encourage a senior leader to begin to reinforce candor?

3. How can you help the situation if one leader is a narcissist and the other is not?

23

Bullies

"I realized that bullying never has to do with you. It's the bully who's insecure."

Shay Mitchell

In this chapter you will learn:

- We are all bullies at some level—some of us more than others.
- Bullies are insecure and are acting out of habit.
- Bullying behavior gets much worse during a discontinuity.
- There are lots of ways to help bullies if they want to be helped.

Another character that is highly disruptive in any organization is the bully. Bullying has become ubiquitous in our society. We see forms of it in every area from the schoolyard to Congress, from the boardroom to the bar. We universally abhor the behavior in school kids, yet we often see it practiced unchallenged by adults. In a transition, the intensity of issues often brings out the worst in bully managers. This chapter will explain bullying and the problems it can cause in a major transition.

Insights About Bullies

So much has been written about bullies. First, understand that the term applies to a continuum of behaviors. On the weak end, we are all bullies, and on the acute end, the mega bully is well known by all. It takes two people for a bullying situation to occur. I may disagree with someone and say so. That person may or may not feel bullied regardless of the method of expressing disagreement. This is because each person has a different level of tolerance when it comes to what constitutes abuse. You and I may hear our manager express a contrary opinion about what we want to do. You may accept the opinion as the manager being open and I may view the statement as being abusive.

John Wooden, the famous basketball coach at UCLA, once said, "We have to learn to disagree without being disagreeable." The problem is that being disagreeable is a term equally defined by the actions of the bully and the perceptions of the victim.

In a bully situation at work, it is sometimes unclear what the true source of the problem is. For example, in *The Bully Free Workplace*, Gary and Ruth Namie discuss the role of upper management as follows: "We've been tough on executives with our candor that they need to stop coddling friends who are bullies. We even invited them to gauge whether or not they are the problem themselves" (2011, 122).

It is easy to recognize extreme bullying. It can cause people to melt down and has been the root cause of many suicides. The feeling of helplessness on the part of the victim becomes so unbearable that death seems to be a more pleasant alternative. Many students spend sleepless nights thinking they would rather die than have to face the bully at school the next day. In some tragic cases, they take action on that thought pattern.

Why people bully is a complex question. If it did not work consistently, then it would not be done for long. However, the bully found out at a very early age that making a big fuss with threatening tones or gestures actually did produce the result he was seeking.

If you take it to the extreme, we are all bullies. Whether you are a bully or not is defined by two things: how extreme your current set of behaviors is relative to getting your way and the reaction in the mind of the victim.

It is well known that some managers and supervisors tend to bluster or become bellicose in order to get people to do their bidding. This is a direct carryover from the playground experience and it normally works. If it does not work, then the bully manager increases the volume until it does. The bully is terrified of the thought: "What if they call my bluff and it doesn't work, what will I do?" While the methodology is intimidation, the basis for bullying is really insecurity. Because stability is gone in times of transition, the bully becomes even more disruptive during a time of organizational change.

Bullies have a negative impact on trust because they push people around mentally and sometimes physically. The most common reaction to a bully is fear and fear is incompatible with trust. To improve trust, you need to find ways to reduce the intimidation effect.

In a transition, we have a set of different ingredients that amplify the desire to bully. Let's examine a few of these special conditions and suppose the bully's response.

Situation	Bully's response
Conditions are not normal, everything is more critical because there is so much to do and so few resources.	"If I am louder people respond faster."
There are new and unknown people lurking around.	"I should establish my territory and let them know I mean business."
Processes are changing and clarity is lacking.	"I must make sure people do not mess with my area."
My job could be cut.	"I should appear to be important and indispensable."
We may be merging with another group.	"I must establish my territory and authority from the start."
People are on edge and nervous.	"I cannot show any vulnerability."
Different people are watching me.	"I must appear to be in full control of the situation."

Unions

A special case of the bullying issue occurs with union officials whose job is to be the watchdog for the employee perspective. This often means playing an adversarial role to the flow of organizational change. Working to integrate these individuals into the process in ways that do not disrupt progress can produce a loss of trust in both directions. If you have unions involved in the reorganization, your work will be much more convoluted. Plan on extra time and anticipate more complexity in the whole process.

In addition to complicating things, the unions add non-value-adding management jobs, which raise the costs of operations. They also create significant work for lawyers. You have to pay the salaries of the union officials and the people who work for them, including the lawyers and the people who work for them. That cost is paid for out of union dues, which lower the standard of living for the workers. So, the union officials bid up the salaries so the workers don't take the brunt of their expenses, but that makes the organization less able to compete.

The story of Hostess Bakeries' bankruptcy and subsequent closing in 2012 is a good example. In an article in the *Atlantic*, "Who's to Blame for the Hostess Bankruptcy, Wall Street, Unions, or Carbs?" Jordan Weissmann wrote: "After failing to win major contract concessions from one of its key labor unions, the beleaguered 82-year-old company has asked a federal bankruptcy court for permission to start liquidating its assets—or, in real person speak, begin the process of selling off pieces of the company to the highest bidder while laying off most of its 18,500 workers." The bankruptcy was due to a number of factors, but the union problems made it impossible for the company to recover, so it closed.

Recognizing a Bully

Few bullies operate that way because they really want to hurt people. Occasionally you can find an individual who delights in making other people miserable, but she may have a mental disorder and could benefit from some help. Most often the bully operates aggressively because she has found that it is the most efficient way to get things accomplished. She probably recognizes that she is often short with people, but thinks that they need her direction to perform up to expectations. Most of the time the bully believes she is doing the logical thing to accomplish her objectives. So how can a bully recognize she is a bully?

Table 23.1: Am I a Bully?

	Yes	No
Do I sometimes lose my temper with others?		
When I am upset, do I tend to raise my voice?		
Have other people asked me to calm down or relax?		
Do I have to stop myself from hitting another person physically?		
Has my boss ever talked to me about being less intense with people?		
Do I feel afraid that people will not do what I want them to do?		
Do people need to be threatened in order to get things done?		
Do I need to apologize sometimes for coming on too strong?		
Do I sense that people are avoiding me?		
Am I excluded from meetings that I should be attending?		
Do people jump when I tell them what to do?		

Bullies Can Change

If you answered "yes" to three or more of the questions in Table 23.1, how can you begin to act differently? How can you act in a more empowering way? Increasing awareness is the key.

- **You must want help.** The first realization is that by bullying other people you are really indicating a need for help yourself. That can be a scary thought, but you must realize that help can make it better for yourself and everyone you work with.

- **Be more alert to your own feelings.** If you frequently feel anxious or nervous about getting things done through other people, it means that you are seeing a need to intervene in order to get people to perform. A great question to ask is "what would happen if I do not intervene?"

- **Log the number of times a day when you feel anger.** You may simply flash at other people out of anger. You do not see it coming, but all of a sudden you blow up at people. Record the number of times this happens in an average day. Some training in anger management may be a good investment to improve your life and the lives of those around you.

- **Ask people.** Ask people if they are feeling bullied. It is a simple question and one that you can test from time to time. Obviously people may be afraid to tell you the truth, so it is important to include body language in the inquiry. If they say "no" but their body language says "yes," listen more to the latter.

- **Ask for a 360-degree evaluation.** There are numerous leadership personality evaluations that will reveal bullying tendencies. It might be a huge wakeup call. In suggesting a 360-degree evaluation, you need to ensure anonymity or the evaluation will be seriously flawed.

- **Have a chat with HR.** If you have bully tendencies, the HR manager will be aware of it through discussions with your subordinates. Say you are aware you have a problem and ask the HR manager what resources might be available to help you.

Ten Skills to Teach a Bully

If you are the supervisor or coach of a bully manager, there are numerous ways to get him to change his behaviors, if he is willing to work with you. You need to gain his cooperation, because success relies on his willingness to participate in a process. Use these ideas in any combination and add your own.

Use the Golden Rule

If the situation were turned around, the bully would not want to be treated the way he is treating others. By reminding the bully of this, the coach can help him see how his actions are being interpreted and how they are hurting other people. This is the start of an awareness campaign. The golden rule is so simple, but it can be powerful medicine in the case of a bully. It may help wake him up. The helpful part of this approach is that you are not scolding the bully and saying "you are a terrible person," rather you are just pointing out that he would not respond well if he were treated the way he is treating other people.

Observe Body Language

People will back away when confronted by a bully. Having the bully pay more attention to the body language of people around him will help him see the reactions in others even if they are too afraid to tell him. Fear is easy to recognize in body language. A facial expression indicating fear will have: eyebrow muscles contract to pull the eyebrows up and in, lower eyelids contract and upper eyelids rise slightly, and lip corners pull sideways tightening and elongating the mouth. Teach the bully to look for these signals. Make sure to couple this awareness building with some of the other sensitivity skills on this list to avoid misuse.

Be More Sensitive to Feedback

Denial is part of the bully's nature. He usually does not see himself as doing anything wrong or unusual. Teach him to be sensitive to feedback from others when they are feeling pushed around, threatened, steam-rolled, judged, or beat up. All these words are signals of people trying to convey that they are feeling bullied. See if the bully can be less aggressive and demonstrate being kind, patient, understanding, or cheerful.

Speak Softly and Slowly

The bully works on emotion and when emotions run high her voice will become louder and the cadence faster. Teach the bully to take a deep breath and speak at half her normal pace with half the volume. Make it a game where the bully actually sees a sound wave in her mind's eye with a volume control. Tell her to turn down the volume, especially when excited or upset.

Ask for Opinions

By seeking the opinions of others, the bully is indicating a willingness to listen. As Stephen Covey wrote in *The Seven Habits of Highly Successful People*, "Seek first to understand and then to be understood" (2004, 237). The bully needs to internalize and practice this advice.

Think Before Speaking

This is really about emotional intelligence. Bullies usually have low EQ because they cannot control their own emotions and they fail to see how they are impacting others. The EQ skill that will help the bully most is to build in a delay between stimulus and response. The delay time is needed for the signal to pass from the limbic system in the brain, which is in the right hemisphere, through the corpus callosum to the logic, or left side of the brain. Building this delay allows a person to think about the consequences of a reaction before doing something. It is one way to improve a person's EQ.

Reduce Use of Absolutes

When we use absolutes (always, never, nobody, not) in our sentences, they make our language sound judgmental. If I said, "You never clean your room," all you need to do is think of one time when you did clean up to reveal me as a liar. Absolutes are confrontational. Teach the bully to use softer terms like rarely, seldom, or perhaps.

Listen More Than Talk

Simply changing the ratio of how much the bully is talking versus listening will help. Bullies are poor listeners. They want to bark out their orders and have other people respond immediately. Teach the bully how to actively listen, especially when the other person is upset or afraid.

Be Kind and Fair

Appealing to the bully's nobler instincts to not pound on a defenseless person may be helpful in some cases. Get the bully to say these words, "unkind and unfair" several times a day to remind him that he needs to change his manner toward others. As a coach, you can ask the bully questions like, "Do you think that exchange came across as unkind?" or, "Do you think you were being unfair when you cut her off in midsentence?" The objective is to increase awareness.

Write Your Own Eulogy

This is a wonderful technique for coaching hardcore bullies. The idea is to actually write down what you would want people to say about you at your funeral. After she writes some things about herself that sound nice, you can say "What are the chances if you died tomorrow that anyone would say those words about you? Would you like to change how others see you?" This technique can be a wake up call for a bully.

There are many more coaching techniques that will help a bully wake up and see the impact she is having on other people. The interesting thing is that if an extreme bully can change just a little bit, the flood of positive energy she will get from other people will encourage her to change even more.

What to Do If You Are Being Bullied

What can the people who are being bullied do to help improve their situation? It boils down to broadening their perspective on the situation. Here are some ideas that may help.

Call Out the Bullying Behavior

One way to push back on a bully is to use the word when it comes up. You can say, "There is no need to bully the staff about this issue." Since the bully is probably not aware that she is one, using the specific word lets the manager know that she crossed the line. This accusation would probably be rejected by the bully, but if the word is used often, the bully may begin to take notice and seek help.

You Cannot Be Bullied If You Do Not Take Offense

Recognize that your perception of being bullied is part of the problem. In many cases, the manager is only trying to get things done and just has a crude way of expressing it. If you did not take offense, then the behavior would not constitute bullying. The victim sees the entire problem as the bully's issue. In fact, there are two sides to every bullying situation. By not taking offense, you can beat the bully at his own game. I am not suggesting this is a "cure" in every case, but I am saying that the problem is never unilateral.

Recognize the Insecurity

Be aware that when a manager bullies people, it is often out of insecurity. You may be able to find ways to help the bully feel like the situation is under control and that his intervention is not required. Look for the underlying motive for why the manager is being a bully. Try to help her understand that if her objective is to make things work more smoothly there is probably a better way to accomplish that.

The Bully Supervisor

A special case of feeling bullied is if you feel your direct supervisor is the bully. All of the techniques listed will apply to this situation, but the intensity of your feeling of being intimidated is more intense because your livelihood is in the balance. In this case there is more of a tendency to hold back and take the abuse. It is this feeling that gives the bully manager his power to manipulate. In some extreme cases, the most effective strategy is to grin and bear it, but usually some combination of the ideas listed above can help reduce your agony. The way out of a bullying situation is individual and situational, so no set of overarching rules can be applied to every situation. You must use judgment, patience, and great wisdom in dealing with a bully boss.

Summary

In persistent cases, you may want to seek help from an ombudsman or HR. These resources can heighten awareness and have impact where an individual subordinate may not have enough power.

In a merger, you may have different supervisors and a variety of different people working for you in rapid succession. The organization structure is quite fluid during the transition, which makes the advice in this chapter more relevant and important.

Food for Thought

1. Describe a time recently when your actions might be considered bullying.

2. How do you react when you are the victim of a bully?

3. What tools can you use to hold up a mirror to a bully and let her see how she is impacting other people?

24

Passive Aggressive People

"A passive approach to professional growth will leave you by the wayside."

Tom Peters

In this chapter you will learn:

- You cannot save everyone, but there are some passive aggressive people who can be turned into superstars.

- Follow the eight suggestions to help draw out a passive aggressive person you really want to save.

- Do not spend a lot of time trying to convert those who will never change.

There is a spectrum of attitudes that crop up in merger situations. The passive aggressive approach is a common problem that is dangerous because of its subtle nature. Passive aggressive people are defiant, but not in an overt way. They undermine rather than support and procrastinate on every action. It is essential to deal with these people in a way that forces them to get with the program or leave. This chapter will provide ideas about how to accomplish this.

Tips for Dealing With Passive Aggressive People

The reasons people become passive aggressive are not as easy to trace as the cause of bullying. If a bully blusters at someone to get his way, the passive aggressive holds her breath until people are ready to listen. Passive aggressive people are usually not violent or loud; in fact, they are the opposite of those things, but they still are behaving in ways opposite to what is expected. The passive aggressive person may work alone or may travel in a group of others with similar tendencies, finding strength and comfort in being around people with similar viewpoints. They take on a cynical and negative attitude to every initiative that is suggested, yet rarely come up with alternative proposals of their own. Every idea suggested is stupid, worthless, or a waste of time. A big problem with these people is that they tend to bring down other individuals who otherwise might be supportive workers. In this way, they act like a virus or cancer on the culture.

In a reorganizing sequence, these individuals indicate support of the effort, but subtly undermine progress at every turn. If they refuse all efforts to change their behavior, then the organization would be better off going forward without them. However, if they are smart enough to realize there is probably going to be a downsizing they will do just enough to not be selected to leave.

The remedy here is to find ways to get them honestly involved in the process. Basically the boss has to earn the trust of the employee step by step. Because the passive aggressive employee is skeptical of anything proposed by management, it takes a lot of consistent behavior to create a different mindset. This is a process where a lot of testing will be done by the employee and the manager needs to pass nearly all of the tests in order to gain the full trust of the passive aggressive employee. Here are some tips that may help get the person on board.

Get to Know Her Personally

The passive aggressive employee gets her power through isolation from management. This does not mean isolation from her peers, as she may be a popular negative force with the other workers. Once you get to know a person on a deeper level you can perhaps begin to understand what makes her resist. Try to meet with her on her own turf rather than in your office. Make it a point to visit with her regularly to find out what is happening with her.

Find Out His Dreams and Passions

Everyone has a key to becoming engaged. If you can find out what he wants out of life, then you may be able to demonstrate how the work he is doing relates to those dreams. For example, the person may be logy and uncooperative at work, merely doing the tasks for which he gets paid. In the course of getting to know him, you may find out that his passion is for baking and particularly for baking dishes from other countries. You would never know of this passion if you were not close to him.

Now you might suggest that the organization create a cultural center where people could display artifacts from their home country or part of our country. It could be a place to chat about local customs and take breaks as an alternative to the sterile break room provided by the company. You might also suggest that he organize a monthly culture appreciation day where everyone who is interested could bring in a dish to share from a selected country's cuisine. This would be the perfect forum for him to show off his baking skills and get him engaged in something positive for the unity of the organization. This situation actually occurred during a reorganization I was involved with, and the cultural center became a significant improvement in the culture of that work area.

Seek Her Opinions

One of the reasons a passive aggressive person checks out is because she is convinced that nobody in management cares about her. If she is specifically asked to voice her ideas and those ideas are at least considered, she may begin to warm up to the group and start to participate.

Give Him a Real Assignment With Autonomy

A passive aggressive person generally does not do well with menial functions within the group. He will do these things, but carry a grudge. Instead, carve out a significant and visible part of the work that you can make his territory. He will do the work and everyone will see the result. Fostering a sense of pride in craftsmanship is one excellent tool for engaging a passive aggressive employee.

Surround Her With Upbeat People

If left to her own devices, the passive aggressive employee will fade into the crowd of others with a similar mindset. In some situations it is difficult to place people in a specific group, but often there is some flexibility by putting the person in another location for a while or changing shifts. The idea is to break up a clique of passive aggressive workers so the more upbeat people can apply some peer pressure.

Give Him Appropriate Recognition

The word appropriate is very important in this tip. You should not give recognition if it is not earned, doing that will feed the wrong behavior. Find out if the person likes his feedback to be public or private and use that method. Often a passive aggressive person will not want to be recognized in public and doing so will actually create more difficulties than you are eliminating.

Get Her Involved in Designing the Transition

Since the transition plan is all about who will do what as the reorganization progresses, there is real power and prestige in being selected to serve on the design team. This appointment also forces involvement with the more positive forces in the community, which will naturally bring out more enthusiasm.

Review His Development Plan

Everyone should have some form of development plan. Make sure he has one that is current and well understood. A great way to keep a passive aggressive employee involved and engaged is for him to see that there is a sincere interest in developing him to reach his full potential. The key reason a passive aggressive employee checks out is because he thinks nobody cares.

Demonstrate Trust in Her

Show real belief that she is capable of excellent work and will do the right thing without being hounded. There are hundreds of opportunities to demonstrate that you trust an individual. Seek them out. Be willing to take what (at the time) may seem as a risk and most of the time the employee will rise to the occasion. Extending trust almost always elicits trustworthy behavior.

Summary

You would not want to spend the effort and time to use all of these actions on a person who is not worth saving. Some people are not going to change no matter how much you try. It is important to figure out who the key resources are that you want to save and develop, then go after them in a positive way. Do not spend your time worrying about the few people you don't believe can be changed. Focus on the people with potential, but do not underestimate that potential. Most people are salvageable with the right mentoring and care. Here is a story of a real person in a real situation, but I will change the names.

Margaret was an informal leader in Mike's department. She was popular at the break room table before work and during breaks and lunch. People listened to Margaret because she was loud, funny, very opinionated, smart, and a natural leader. Margaret was also very much anti-establishment going into a merger of departments.

Margaret was an activist in her circle, but very passive in her work habits. She was apathetic at department meetings. She once told Mike in a public meeting that there were so many problems in his department that he was "lucky to be in business."

I decided that Margaret could be an exceptional employee because of her great personal characteristics, if only I could get her head pointed in the right direction. I secretly adopted Margaret. I would sit with her in the break room a couple times a week to chat. It was uncomfortable at first, but I kept doing it. I learned what made her tick.

With Mike's help, I found ways to draw Margaret into the circle of decision makers for the integration process. Using the tips outlined in this chapter, I slowly found ways to reduce the passive aggressive behaviors and an amazing metamorphosis occurred over a period of about six months.

By the end of the first year of the integration, we promoted Margaret to be the supervisor of a group. Her natural leadership abilities were harnessed for the benefit of the organization, and she was a vocal advocate for the turnaround in the department that she helped to create. Margaret could easily see her huge contribution and was genuinely proud of it. She was a shining star and turned out to be one of our stronger supervisors.

Imagine the power of turning a highly negative and influential person into a strong advocate. That kind of leverage is possible by converting a passive aggressive employee into a superstar employee.

Food for Thought

1. What is another idea about how you could get closer to a person in the work setting?

2. What percentage of negative and passive workers do you think are worth trying to change?

3. Often the initial efforts to adopt a worker are rejected because of lack of trust. How would you deal with that situation?

25

People in Denial

"We live in a world of denial, and we don't know what the truth is anymore."

Javier Bardem

In this chapter you will learn:

- Denial is the most common reaction to a reorganization.
- The best way to deal with denial is to communicate the change in ways that allow venting.
- When people are in deep grief, do not try to cheer them up with predictions of a brighter future. It may backfire.

When human beings are exposed to a great shock, they have a defense mechanism called denial. When a parent loses a child to a tragic accident, it is common for the parent to be unable to believe what has just happened. Sometimes, in severe cases, the denial can go on for months or even years. The same phenomenon happens when people experience the shock of their professional world being turned upside down.

Some people will carry on in a kind of suspended animation of denial. These individuals are not bad; they simply have trouble getting with the program and they are operating among other individuals who are in full panic mode. The cure for denial is a different and more robust communication pattern. A leader's actions during the initial roll out can either facilitate or stifle the grieving process.

I remember announcing a highly unpopular reorganization where I made a big mistake and learned an important lesson about denial. The situation occurred in a department that had been doing exceptionally well under a leader I will call John. I was the division manager and John reported to me. He had been in charge for about three years and the people loved his open style. He had the entire workforce aligned behind his vision, and they were performing very well against some very tough goals. John was a super leader, but he had a flaw when viewed by upper management. He was protective of his culture and did not want his department to participate in some progressive initiatives being pushed from the top. He perceived that the changes would result in less control by him.

John took an insular approach with the initiatives, coming up with all kinds of reasons why his area should be excluded from the larger change process. This resistance made him even more popular with his people, because they saw him as their protector from the big bad change agents at the top. I observed the push and pull that was going on between my direct report and my own manager and tried to coach John to soften his resistance. He did not. I was finally asked by my manager to move John to a different role because he was in denial about what had to be done.

I was nervous about a transition of leaders in this department because of its tremendous performance and the equity John had with the people. Talking with my superiors, I agreed to replace John on the condition that I was allowed to pick an even stronger leader to take his place. Finally, after some tricky negotiations, I was able to secure Mary, who had an exceptional reputation as a leader and was an upcoming superstar in the organization. I was thrilled to have Mary replace John, because it really was time for a change, and this was a good leadership change. I also ensured that John found a good place to land where he could continue to grow and gain influence. His resistance had done damage to his reputation and I wanted to get him the best possible pathway to a brighter future.

I still remember the day I called the department group together (it was a shift operation, so we had about 40 people on the day shift at the meeting). I announced that John would be moving to another job and that Mary would be replacing him at the end of the week. As I looked out over the sea of faces, I saw shock and disbelief. The grief quickly turned to anger when I tried to make the situation better with logic. Here is what I told the group:

"I know that you all enjoy working for John. He has been here a few years and you really love his leadership style. Your performance under John has been super and management really appreciates what you and he have done here. I can also see that my decision to replace John and bring in Mary is not a happy announcement for any of you. Let me make a prediction here. I believe that six months from now you will all enjoy working for Mary even more than you have enjoyed working for John. Mary is a seasoned leader with a great track record."

Looking back on that little speech, I can see it was a wonder they let me out of the room with my head still on. The group was furious with me. Not only did I make a bad decision in their eyes, but I had insulted them by suggesting that the new person would be better than their favorite manager. That was a particularly low point in my tenure as a division manager of 12 departments.

The most significant mistake I made in the announcement was not allowing the group to grieve before trying to convince them that things would be better in the future. They were in denial of the change and in no mood for some logic from me. It was an ugly scene. I learned a lesson about trying to change people's opinions when they are in denial and grieving for the past. If I had let them know that John was going to be leaving and we would deal with a successor soon, they would have been sad and depressed, but perhaps not so angry about it.

My prediction was actually correct, except it did not take six months for Mary to win them over. Within three months I had people thanking me for the move I had made and saying how much better Mary was than her predecessor. The key point that stayed with me is to be careful about trying to make people feel better with logic. Let them grieve and make them feel better in the long run with your actions.

The other action to take is to communicate the message through many different channels. People will find denial harder to maintain if they experience the input in five different ways over a period of a few days. Make sure you use different communication channels with your multiple messages. For example, you might start with a personal announcement given in a town hall format that includes the opportunity for questions, then you could follow up with a video discussion of the significance of the change and how it will have a positive impact on the organization.

You could bolster that content in an open question and answer session on the Internet and arrange a series of live chats online. For a large or complex change, you could follow up with a physical letter to the individuals involved. Even voicemail is helpful at reaching some people, especially if they are in remote locations. The idea is to find creative ways for people to hear a consistent message along with an open channel for them to ask questions or comment. Taking the time to communicate in this way will pay off because fewer people will remain in denial and more will get busy helping to build the future.

Food for Thought

1. What are the physical symptoms of people who are in denial? How about grief?

2. People go through the grief process at different rates. How do you accommodate the needs of both the fast recovery people and those who take longer to adjust to the change?

3. Is there ever a case where you might retrench and reverse your decisions about the change? What are the dynamics involved in a decision like this?

26

Wheeler Dealers

"So many things happen for every event, and if you try to manipulate it, it means you are struggling against the whole universe, and that's just silly."

Deepak Chopra

In this chapter you will learn:

- Lobbying for the best deal is a human trait.
- If someone is over the top with making side deals, the best defense is exposure.
- Suggestions to help control the problem.

In every crowd, you will find people who are very crafty at finding the best solution for their own interests. This is human nature and we will all instinctively do some of this. In a transition, you will likely find some individuals who take the behavior to an unhealthy extreme and you need to be prepared to deal with them effectively.

Whenever there is chaos, individuals will instinctively look at self-preservation as the highest ordered need. We cannot stop this process because it is built into our DNA. People quickly understand what is in their long-term best interest, even amid chaos. Some people try to game the system even when there is no formal system to game. They will set up mini pockets of rules that allow them to remain as safe as possible while the battle rages about them. It is the same force that drives people into storm shelters during a tornado. Leaders need to recognize that the shelters set up by different people will vary and inevitably be incompatible with each other and with the new order.

The wheeler dealer is usually a highly social individual who tries to rally support for a side process that is favorable to him or his group, but that may not fit with the overall idea of the reorganization. For example, Pete works in the credit department of a bank. He is aware that his department is going to be consolidated with the credit department in another bank across town during the merger of the two banks. As soon as the announcement was made, Pete contacted one of the people in the other credit department to arrange a lunch in order to figure out how many people they are likely to need. The manager of the credit department is already having discussions with both bank presidents relative to staffing levels, so Pete's side effort is going to do nothing but make confusion. Still, Pete feels it is in his best interest to at least suggest some alternate ideas to his manager.

I call this type of behavior "meddling." The person inserts himself in a process where he has not been invited and is not welcome. After a while, there are two competing processes going on and some effort must be made to clear the air.

During the transition phase of any change initiative, there is going to be some bargaining going on. That is one of the hallmarks of the transition phase. If employees are blocked from getting better offices, they will bargain for more convenient parking. If employees are going to have to work on an upper floor, they will try to locate their cubicle near the elevators. The list of desires is a mile long and every individual rightfully wants to lobby for the best possible deal.

The problem is when one individual takes the actions to an extreme and starts to cut pseudo-deals that he has no authority to make. Then chaos erupts. People hear rumors about the deal that Pete has supposedly struck and demand equality. Bargaining is a part of the classic grieving process.

This phenomenon is like kids at a playground, all trying to be the first to get served at the ice cream truck. You will observe jockeying for position at first, followed by some more serious pushing and shoving that may eventually break out into fistfights, depending on the particular individuals in the group. The same kind of dynamic happens in a work transition, but, instead of the ice cream truck, it becomes "who is going to have the office with a window."

For many years I worked at a company where the buildings in manufacturing were brick construction with very few windows. Having an office with a window was a coveted status symbol. One executive dreamed of having a window, but always ended up in an internal office with no windows at all. He finally got so frustrated that he commissioned an artist to paint a picture of a window and hung it on the wall in his office. The executive could not get what he wanted by natural means, so he acted like a wheeler dealer and made a side deal to get it anyway. It was a childish response that lowered the executive's esteem within the community. That kind of behavior goes on in every transition, and we need to be sure to minimize it. Let's examine some ideas for how to reduce the bargaining:

- **Establish a behavioral expectation of equality.** Let people know that there will be a fair process that will consider the needs of everyone and that individuals trying to set up rules or agreements for their own benefit are not appreciated.

- **Make peer pressure work.** Group pressure will try to make a level playing field in terms of working conditions or other perks. Have the group police itself with an attitude of people working together rather than individuals out for themselves.

- **Have extreme wheeler dealers sit on the decision committee.** People inclined to grab the goodies for themselves who suddenly find themselves in a group that needs to decide what is fair, will find their greed diluted by exposure.

- **Set up a system that some perks are earned.** Let the plum offices go to those people who deserve them by how hard they work, not by which political allies they were able to influence.

- **Have a democratic decision process.** Put critical decisions up for a vote by the affected population. This process might be combined by a management veto provision to prevent abuse.

- **Let people know you trust them to do what is fair and right.** Extending trust will cause those who might be selfish to think twice about working against the greater good.

- **Have a candid talk with the worst offenders.** A wheeler dealer likes to work in the shadows and will be embarrassed if exposed. Let the person know that his actions are being noticed and that further lobbying will not be appreciated.

- **Reward selfless gestures.** If people who favor the more equitable route are celebrated, then the wheeler dealer is going to sink further into the background. He will not want to be discovered looking out for his own interests when his neighbor is being rewarded for being selfless.

None of these actions are foolproof, but they will push things in the right direction, especially if they are applied consistently and overtly. The more transparent the decision system, the less room there is for a wheeler dealer to operate without being detected. The clandestine nature of the wheeler dealer's operation provides the best opportunity to control it.

Food for Thought

1. What other methods might work to dampen the efforts of a wheeler dealer?

2. How would you draw the line between normal self-interest and inappropriate selfish behavior?

3. How would you set limits and higher expectations for a wheeler dealer?

27

Gossip Mongers

*"People love gossip. It's the biggest thing that keeps
the entertainment industry going."*

Ellen DeGeneres

In this chapter you will learn:

- Rumors and gossip are part of the human condition.
  They are going to exist.

- The best defense for rumor is to build an environment
  of high trust.

- There are many other antidotes to excessive rumors
  and gossip.

- The issue of rumors and gossip is rooted in fear.
  Eliminating the fear through good communication
  will reduce the problem.

Nature hates a vacuum. In the absence of reliable and timely information,

human beings will invent information to fill the void. If you have a bare

spot in the lawn, nature will fill it in quickly, usually with weeds. If you

take a pail of water out of a pond, nature will fill it in immediately so no hole exists in the surface. So it is with people. When there is a vacuum of credible information, people fill in the situation with information of their invention, usually weeds. They do not often cause irreversible harm, but they waste a lot of time and energy on idle chatter that could be avoided. It is best to deal with these people directly. The antidote to rumors and gossip is trust, along with better and more frequent communication of the truth, even if it is unsettling information.

Controlling Gossip

The following are some ideas that can help control situations where there is too much gossip. Realize that the most important antidote by far is the first one—building trust.

Build Trust

Rumors have a hard time gaining traction in an environment of high trust because there is credibility in the information that is shared and if there is a question, people bring it to the attention of their manager.

Intervene Quickly

Act quickly when there is a rumor and as much as possible provide solid, believable information about what is really going to happen. It is best to have this intervention before the rumor even starts, but it is essential to nip the problem as soon as it is detected.

Coach the Worst Offenders to Stop

Usually it is not hard to tell which people like to stir up trouble. They are easy to spot in the break room. Take these people aside and ask them to tone down the speculation. One interesting way to mitigate a group of gossipers is to sit at the lunch table with them. This may feel uncomfortable at first, but it can be very helpful for detecting rumors early. Just like fighting a disease, the sooner the treatment can be applied, the easier the problem is to control.

Double the Communication

There are times when the genesis of a rumor is easy to predict. Suppose all the top managers attend a long closed-door meeting with the shades pulled. People are going to wonder what is being discussed. Suppose the financial performance indicates that continuing on the present path is impossible. What if there are strange people walking around the shop floor with tape measures? There could be a consultant going around asking all kinds of probing questions. All these things, and numerous others, are bound to drive people to start speculating. When this happens, smart leaders interact more with the people. Unfortunately, when there are unusual circumstances, most managers like to hide in their offices or in meetings to avoid having to deal with pointed questions, which is not helpful.

Find Multiple Ways to Communicate the Truth

People need to hear something more than once to believe it. According to the Edelman Trust Barometer for 2011, nearly 60 percent of people indicate they need to hear organizational news (good or bad) at least three to five times before they believe it. Communicate through town hall meetings, newsletters, e-mails, voicemail, texting, small group meetings, even posters.

Reinforce Open Dialogue

If people are praised rather than punished for speaking out when there are questions or disconnects, they will do more of it. Open, honest dialogue is a short circuit to the rumor mill. It also helps build trust, which is the best way to subdue the rumor agents.

Model a No-Gossip Policy

People pick up on the tactics of a leader and mimic them. If the leader is prone to sending out juicy bits of unsubstantiated speculation, then others in the organization will be encouraged to do the same. Conversely, if a leader refuses to discuss information that is potentially incorrect, she is modeling the kind of self-control that will be picked up by at least some people.

Summary

I would caution against having managers try to manipulate the rumor mill by spreading rumors of their own. I knew one manager who used to plant false rumors by leaking out a little misinformation. The idea was like trying to set a backfire to burn off the fuel in order to help control a forest fire. It is extremely dangerous to attempt.

Trust and rumors are mostly incompatible. If there is low trust, it is easy for someone to project a negative idea of the future. When trust is low, these sparks can create a roaring blaze like a lit cigarette in a dry forest. If trust is high, the spark may still be there, but it will have trouble catching because people will just check with the boss about the validity of the rumor.

When trust is high, the communication process is efficient, as leaders share valuable insights about business conditions and strategy to the extent they legally can. In low trust organizations, rumors and gossip zip around the organization like laser beams in a hall of mirrors. Before long, leaders are blinded by problems coming from every direction. Trying to control the rumors takes energy away from the mission and strategy and does not serve customer needs.

Each person is different and will react in ways that make sense to him. Dealing with all the different voices is what makes leadership challenging and fun. It is beyond the scope of this book to go into all possible personality types to offer solutions. The previous few chapters dealt with the most common forms of disruptive behavior, but this is far from an exhaustive list. Regardless of the aberration, the prime resolution is to focus efforts on enhancing trust. When an individual becomes calcified or unable to respond, it is time for that person to move on. Investing too much time on lost causes will prevent forward progress.

Food for Thought

1. If you were the manager and heard a juicy rumor from the staff, how would you deal with it?

2. What would happen if you confronted a person spreading a rumor and asked him to stop?

3. Suppose someone suggested spreading a false rumor. What would be the advantages and ethical issues of doing this?

Part VI:

Wrap Up

This final section brings together the key points that will help you run a successful change initiative. We have discussed a more balanced approach to reorganizations, restructurings, mergers, and acquisitions that aims to satisfy all of the stakeholders. Leaders who follow these ideas will have a better chance of meeting their goals for reorganization, because the approach will lead to higher trust throughout the organization.

28

Final Considerations

"Everything can be taken from a man but one thing: the last of human freedoms—to choose one's attitude in any given set of circumstances, to choose one's own way."

Viktor E. Frankl

In this chapter you will learn:

- The key points that make a successful change initiative.
- Trust is the most important ingredient in a successful organization.

Whether you are in the middle of integrating an acquisition, contemplating a merger in the next few years, or making a significant reorganization, you need to be aware of the minefield you are entering when you embark on this change. You and your team will be tested beyond what you thought possible to endure, and you will need the collective muscle of nearly every person on both teams to make the venture successful.

The odds are not in your favor to get through the integration with the kind of environment you really want, but on the flip side, adversity is the best way to test the greatness of a leader. Your patience will be tested, almost daily, and you will need some tools to weather the inevitable setbacks. Let's begin by sharing a list of seven ways to deal with setbacks.

Recovering From Setbacks

Any reorganization is going to be a major transition. I think the metaphor of a journey is quite helpful at laying out some principles we can use when the going gets tough. This section refers to a list coined by Brian Tracy in a timeless speech entitled "Success is a Journey," which was given to a group of 5,000 life insurance salesmen in Toronto in 1989 (used here with the permission of Brian Tracy). These ideas can help you recover from setbacks and reach your goal successfully.

- **Decide on your goal and launch.** Nothing gets done if you only dream about a better future. The first step is the hardest one to take, but all the others follow from that one. Overcoming difficulties means having the courage to start on the journey, realizing it will challenging at times. The very act of getting started is a great positive step toward reaching your goal. It shows that you have the courage to do it.

- **Never consider the possibility of failure.** The mental toughness to persevere when things look completely bleak is exactly the attitude needed. There will be times during the process when it seems the whole venture was a bad idea, and you want to quit. But, as Vince Lombardi once said, "Winners never quit, and quitters never win." The concept of never even considering what will happen if we fail sets us up for success. Leaders need to insist on this kind of posture, so that setbacks will feel more like speed bumps than brick walls.

- **Take it one step at a time.** A setback in the reorganization is just something that went wrong. It is a misstep on the trail that does not doom the journey, unless you let it. Focus on doing the next step well rather than worrying about the entire process. While the whole process looks impossibly complex, each step of the process is quite manageable.

- **Watch out for the naysayers.** Along the way, people will tell you it cannot be done. If you listen to these people and begin to soften your resolve, you will prove them right. Listen to their ideas and helpful suggestions, but do not let them dissuade you from your goal. Success requires fortitude.

- **Obstacles and difficulties come not to obstruct but to instruct.** If you view each setback as a leaning opportunity, you make the process more robust as you go. Do not fear the problems. They will show up from time to time. Just learn from them and move forward. As Napoleon Hill said, "Every adversity, every unpleasant circumstance, every failure, and every physical pain carries with it the seed of an equivalent benefit" (1971, 1).

- **Be clear about your goal, but keep your mind open.** Sometimes setbacks require creative solutions to keep on the path to the overall objective. Make sure you move forward with integrity and allow only ethical solutions, but be sure to encourage creative thinking to navigate around obstacles. Do this by asking "will this action move us toward the goal?" and "is this the best action available?" When you answer yes to both questions, you have the best possible action.

- **Nobody does it alone.** On any journey you need the help of others to meet your goal. That is abundantly clear for reorganization efforts because there are people in the other part of the organization that want it to be successful too. In fact, everyone on the team has a contribution to make to the overall effort. Work together, sweat together, and celebrate together. Above all, trust each other.

Summary

By far, the most important ingredient for a successful integration is trust. If you do not have trust at first, then start building it immediately by following the ideas in this book. Trust is the glue that holds the entire operation together in times of transition. Trust is not granted to leaders, but earned through behavior.

In this book I have discussed a more balanced approach to reorganizations, restructurings, mergers, or acquisitions that aims to satisfy all of the stakeholders. Leaders who follow these ideas will have a better chance of meeting their goals for reorganization, because the approach will lead to higher trust throughout the organization.

You have learned some tested ideas that can improve your odds of success. Since there are thousands of ways to go off track and only a few critical paths that will take you to victory, I offer these ideas to give you some food for thought. This will be a big test for your leadership capability. You can beat the odds if you select a wise path and work diligently toward it.

Appendix: Key Points

Recognize That There Are Two Simultaneous Processes

While the major change process appears to be one rather complex system from the outside, there are actually two distinct processes going on inside. One is the mechanical process to accomplish the new configuration and the other is the people process where the culture reacts to the mechanical process and tries to move from the old configuration to the new one. The most common mistake made in reorganizations is to put too much emphasis on the mechanical side and not enough effort into working on the culture. This limited focus is the primary reason for the dismal track record of reorganization efforts and why they often don't accomplish their goals.

Focus on the Big Picture

Reorganization is a change process. Keep the focus on the big picture or main objective and make sure all activities are moving you toward that goal. It is so easy to get distracted and have some activities take you in the wrong direction.

Avoid Overworking People

Having one person do the work of two people is a formula for burnout. It is possible to combine jobs through reorganization to allow for staffing cuts, but avoid the temptation to ask just one person to take on all the responsibilities of another person who is leaving. Also ensure there is adequate cross training before individuals leave the organization. You cannot afford to let process and customer knowledge walk out the door just because you have decided to downsize.

Satisfy the Customer at All Times

Take care of the customer throughout the process. Quite often in the mad rush to make changes, customer focus is moved to a back burner. This mistake will kill a business faster than anything else. Put significant energy into ensuring exceptional customer focus despite the trauma going on within both entities.

Avoid Management Isolation

Leaders who are trying to arrange and plan the reorganization have much more work to do, so time becomes scarce. Do not neglect your time interacting with employees during this process. They need close contact and daily information and you need to hear firsthand what is going on in the organization as you make decisions. If you become too isolated trying to engineer the process, you and your organization are not going to like what you end up building.

Communicate Twice the Normal Amount

Despite the time shortage, make sure to increase, rather than neglect your communication during all phases of the reorganization. Two-way communication is essential, people need to hear the important messages three to five times before they will believe them.

Pay Special Attention to Frontline Supervision

These people operate at the critical junction between workers and management. They often are not well trained in leadership techniques, yet they need to perform their function flawlessly or the whole change effort will be compromised. The skills and attitudes of these supervisors have a huge impact on the people. Pay special attention to frontline supervisors and train them well.

Integrate the Culture Quickly

Dragging out reorganization is not a good idea, but neither is rushing it. Work to have a crisp project that is well defined ahead of time and properly executed. The longer the process drags on, the greater the probability you will lose valuable customers and employees.

Support HR

Recognize that there is an increased load on everyone in the organization, but HR has the most significant increase. It is a bad idea to reduce headcount in HR just prior to or during the integration. In fact, many groups budget for additional HR resources during integration. After things settle down the HR staff can be reduced.

Use, but Do Not Overuse, Systems Thinking

Many of the tools in systems thinking can help leaders visualize what is going on so a more comprehensive program can be conducted. Select a few tools and use them as long as they are helpful. Avoid the trap where you become obsessed with numerous analyses and checklists. Some tools help in moderation.

Have Some Fun Along the Way

Reorganizing a business is really hard work. There are thousands of ways you can cause yourself problems, which is why so few ventures work out well. It is important to do the work with a positive spirit. Take time to celebrate the progress being made and keep the goal in view at all times. If the work is done well, the results will be worth the effort.

Readiness Evaluation

Circle the level that applies to your situation for each question. It is important to be objective and honest.

What is the level of experience with mergers and acquisitions on your management team?

1. It is the first time out for most or the team.

2. Some people have experience.

3. We have many people on staff who have done this before.

4. We have vast experience doing successful integrations.

Do you believe a merger or acquisition will significantly enhance the performance of your organization?

1. We are not sure it will.

2. We are thinking it may help, but worried about the distraction.

3. We feel it is worth the effort.

4. There is strong commitment from all people.

Have you engaged an outside consultant to help with the process?

1. Not yet, we are still discussing.

2. We are evaluating a couple alternatives.

3. We have selected the firm we intend to use.

4. We have been working with a firm for several months.

Do you have a specific plan to integrate the cultures into one smooth functioning group?

1. Not yet. We will see how it goes and make adjustments as needed.

2. We have many ideas, but no formal plan yet.

3. We have a plan, but it is kind of sketchy.

4. We have a solid plan with contingencies and teams identified.

What is the basis for this expansion?

1. Greater revenue.

2. Expanded product line.

3. Critical mass.

4. All of these things.

What is the degree of cultural fit between these two organizations?

1. They are two very different groups.

2. They are similar but not well aligned.

3. They are different but synergistic.

4. They are highly compatible.

How long to you anticipate it will take for full integration?

1. We have not estimated that.

2. It may take years.

3. It should take less than 2 years.

4. It should take less than 1 year.

Have you articulated a common vision for the merged organization?

1. Not yet, but we are discussing this.

2. We have a team working on this.

3. Vision is generated but not full buy-in yet.

4. The vision is clear and well supported by the entire organization.

Are the company values of both organizations clear and compatible?

1. The values need clarification.

2. The values are not the same ones.

3. Values are there but somewhat vague.

4. The joint values are crystal clear and supported.

Have the expected team behaviors been communicated?

1. Not specifically.

2. The expected behaviors are sketchy.

3. We have expected behaviors, but they are not well understood yet.

4. The behaviors are strong, well communicated, and modeled from the top.

Is the human resources group prepared for the additional workload over an extended period of time?

1. We may downsize the HR group.

2. No, the HR people are already stretched too thin.

3. We will add some temps.

4. Yes, HR is fully staffed for the additional load.

What is the degree of enthusiasm among the management team (including the supervisors)?

1. Hostile.

2. Guarded.

3. Interested and somewhat positive.

4. Enthusiastic and energized.

Do people in the ranks fear this action?

1. Yes, there is significant fear.

2. Some fear, but we are working on that.

3. Not strong fear, but there is some anxiety.

4. Most people welcome this action.

Have you communicated the implications of this change to your customers?

1. Customers are not yet aware this is going to happen.

2. Some customers may be impacted negatively during the transition.

3. Customers will be fine with this change.

4. Customers already see an advantage in what we are doing.

To what degree have you included the owners (shareholders) in the decision to do this?

1. We plan to inform them soon.

2. They are aware and have some concerns.

3. The owners are supportive of this move.

4. The owners have been pushing for this and think it is an excellent move.

Have you done an environmental impact study?

1. No study yet.

2. We expect to do this soon.

3. There are no environmental issues.

4. The study is completed and all issues have been addressed.

Have your vendors and suppliers approved the plan?

1. No, they are not aware yet.

2. They are concerned about the impact on them.

3. They are informed and are supportive.

4. The suppliers and vendors see this as a very good thing for them.

Do you have a documented communications plan for the community in terms of impact?

1. No, we only have ideas at this point.

2. The communications plan is vague but we are working on it.

3. We have hired a communications firm to help with the roll out.

4. The communications plan is in place, and we are using it now.

Have you created a map of the entire process including a timeline?

1. No, we have some ideas, but no firm written map.

2. There are several parts of a plan, but no integrated map.

3. The plan is in progress, but needs some work.

4. The map of the entire process is completed and has been shared with the organization.

Have you set up teams to help with the cultural integration?

1. We still have to do this.

2. We are working on that now.

3. There are several teams that have been assigned.

4. The teams are up and running successfully.

Are there job descriptions for all positions in the merged organization?

1. No, the job descriptions will come later.

2. We have not yet decided on the final structure.

3. The job description process is underway.

4. All job descriptions are completed but may be amended later.

Do you have a training plan set up for all new functions?

1. We are not that well defined.

2. Training will be done when we get the time. There is too much chaos now.

3. Plans are being put in place.

4. The training process is already underway.

Have you made special provision to help the first line supervisors?

1. We do not think this is necessary.

2. We are discussing the impact with supervisors.

3. They have been part of the planning process.

4. We have a proactive support structure for supervisors.

Do you have a retention plan for the people you need to keep on the team?

1. They will stay, no problem.

2. We have informed them.

3. We have a plan to retain the best people.

4. We have a master plan for retention of people at all levels.

Have you started the due diligence process?

1. No, we are still getting started.

2. We are in the data gathering phase.

3. Yes, but there is still a long way to go.

4. Due diligence is on track.

The emphasis of this readiness questionnaire was on the human integration aspects of a merger or acquisition rather than the legal or financial side of the transition.

To score your readiness for the transition, simply add up the score for each of the 27 questions. It will be a more accurate assessment if several different people score the questions independently and then average the scores. See the table below for your results.

Score Range	Implications Readiness
<50	The initiative is too sketchy to be successful. Take more time getting ready.
51-75	You are on the right track, but there are several details to put in place.
76-100	You have a solid plan and are in good shape for this integration.

References

Bardwick, J. and G. Perritt. (1991). *Danger in the Comfort Zone*. New York: AMACOM.

Barker, J.A. (1985). *The Power of Vision*. Burnsville, MN.

Bassman, E. (1992). *Abuse in the Workplace: Management Remedies and Bottom Line Impact*. West Port, CT: Quorum.

Bellingham, R. (2010). *Getting People and Culture Right in Mergers and Acquisitions*. Amherst, MA: HRD Press.

Bennis, W, (1999). *Old Dogs, New Tricks*. Provo, UT: Executive Excellence Publishing.

Bennis, W. (2010). *Still Surprised: A Memoir of a Life in Leadership*. San Francisco: Jossey-Bass.

Bennis, W. (April 2008). "The Art of Followership." Leadership Excellence, 4.

Bennis, W., D. Goleman, and J. O'Toole. (2008). *Transparency: How Leaders Create a Culture of Candor*. San Francisco: Jossey-Bass.

Blanchard, K. (2002). *Whale Done! The Power of Positive Relationships*. New York: The Free Press.

Blanchard, K. (2003). *Servant Leader*, Nashville, TN: Thomas Nelson.

Bradberry, T., and J. Greaves. (2009). *Emotional Intelligence 2.0*, San Diego: TalentSmart.

Buckingham, M. and D. Clifton. (2001). *Now Discover Your Strengths*. New York: The Free Press.

Buono, A.F. and J.L. Bowditch. (2003). *The Human Side of Mergers and Acquisitions: Managing collisions Between People, Cultures, and Organizations*. Washington, DC: BeardBooks.

Byham, W. (1990). *Zapp—The Lightning of Empowerment*. New York: Harmony Books..

Carney, W.J. (2007). *Mergers and Acquisitions: Cases and Materials*. New York: Foundation Press.

Collins, J. (2001). *Good to Great*. New York: Harper Collins.

Connors, R. and T. Smith. (2009). *How Did That Happen: Holding People Accountable for Results The Positive Principled Way*. New York: Portfolio Penguin.

Covey, S. (2000). *The Seven Habits of Highly Effective People*, New York: Running Press.

Covey, S.M.R. (2006). *The Speed of Trust: The One Thing That Changes Everything*. New York: Simon & Schuster.

Covey, S.M.R. and G. Link. (2012). *Smart Trust*. New York: Free Press.

Fisher, K. (1999). *Leading Self-Directed Work Teams: A Guide to Developing New Team Leadership*. New York: McGraw-Hill Professional.

Fishman, R. (2013). "Culture Clash." Slate.

Galpin, T.J. and M. Herndon. *Mergers & Acquisitions: Process Tools to Support M&A Integration at Every Level*. San Francisco: Jossey-Bass.

Gladwell, M. (2005). *Blink*. New York: Little Brown and Company.

Goleman, D. (1994). *Emotional Intelligence*. New York: Bantam Books.

Harari, O. (2003). *The Leadership Secrets of Colin Powell*. New York: McGraw-Hill Professional.

Hill, N. (1971). *You Can Work Your Own Miracles*. New York: Fawcett Books.

Hill, N. (1987). Think and Grow Rich. New York: Ballantine Books.

Hill, N. "The Science of Personal Achievement," Niles, IL: *Nightingale Conant*.

Holson, Laura M. (2006). "Disney Agrees to Acquire Pixar in a $7.4 Billion Deal". *The New York Times*. Retrieved April 22, 2008.

Holtz, L. (1988). "Do Right," *Washington Speakers Bureau*, Alexandria, VA.

Horsager, D. (2009). *The Trust Edge: What Top Leaders Have & 8 Pillars to Build It*, Minneapolis, MN: Leaf River Publishing.

Johnson, S. (1998). *Who Moved My Cheese?* New York: Penguin Putnam.

Kimmel, B.B. (2013). *Trust Inc.: Strategies for Building Your Company's Mast Valuable Asset*, Chester, NJ: Next Decade Inc.

Kotter, J. (2005). *Our Iceberg Is Melting: Changing and Succeeding Under Any Conditions*. New York: St. Martin's Press.

Machiavelli, N. (2003). *The Prince*, Dante University Press.

Mackey, J. and R. Sisodia. (2013). "Conscious Capitalism: Liberating the Heroic Spirit of Business" *Harvard Business Review*.

Maxwell, J. (1991). *The 21 Irrefutable Laws of Leadership*, Nashville TN: Thomas Nielson.

Namie, G. and R. Namie (2011). *The Bully-Free Workplace: Stop Jerks, Weasles, and Snakes From Killing Your Organization*. Hoboken, NJ: John C. Wiley.

Namie, G. and R.F. Namie, (2011) *The Bully Free Workplace*, Hoboken NJ. John C. Wiley.

Nightingale, E. "Lead the Field," *Nightingale Conant*, Niles, IL.

Patterson, K., J. Grenny, R. McMillan, and A. Switzler. (2005). *Crucial Confrontations*. New York: McGraw Hill.

Reina, D. and R. Michelle. (2006). *Trust and Betrayal in the Workplace*. San Francisco: Berrett-Koehler.

Sample, S.B. *The Contrarian's Guide to Leadership*. San Francisco: Jossey-Bass.

Selden, L. and G. Colvin. (2003). "M&A Needn't Be a Loser's Game," *Harvard Business Review*: 70-79.

Senge, P.M. (1990). *The Fifth Discipline: The Art & Practice of The Learning Organization*. New York: Bantam Doubleday.

Siegenthaler, P.J. (2009). *Perfect M&As: The Art of Business Integration*. Cornwall: Ecademy Press.

Stack, J. (2013). *The Great Game of Business* New York: Crown Business.

Stanford, M. (1983). *Management Policy*. Upper Saddle River, NJ: Prentice Hall.

Tracy, B. "Success is a Journey," Brian Tracy International, Solana Beach, CA.

Vanourek, R. and G. (2012). *Triple Crown Leadership: Building Excellent, Ethical, and Enduring Organizations*. New York: McGraw Hill.

Weissmann, J. (2012). "Who's to Blame for the Bankruptcy: Wall Street, Unions, or Carbs?" *The Atlantic*, November 16.

Whipple, R. (2009). *Leading With Trust is Like Sailing Downwind*. Provo, UT: Executive Excellence Publishing.

Whipple, R. *The Trust Factor: Advanced Leadership for Professionals*. Hilton, NJ: Productivity Publications.

About the Author

Bob Whipple is CEO of Leadergrow, an organization dedicated to development of leaders. As a leadership coach and business consultant, he works with individual clients as well as large organizations such as government agencies, corporations, and associations. A highly successful leader at a Fortune 500 company for more than 30 years, Bob accomplished revolutionary change while leading a division of over 2000 people through the application of outstanding people skills.

Bob is a student of the leadership process and has developed unique approaches to achieving excellent results through the full engagement of people. His ability to communicate pragmatic approaches to building trust in an entertaining and motivational format has won him top ranking wherever he works. Audiences relate to his material enthusiastically because it is simple, yet profound. His work has earned him the title of "The Trust Ambassador."

Bob holds a bachelor's degree in mechanical engineering from Union College, a master's degree in chemical engineering from Syracuse University, and a master's of business administration from the Simon School at the University of Rochester. He has achieved a Certified Professional in Learning and Performance (CPLP) certification from the American Society for Training & Development (recertified in 2014).

Bob lives with his wife, Kay, in Hilton, New York, a small town outside of Rochester where he has a "gentleman's farm." He enjoys doing landscaping and gardening, stained glass art, and woodworking.

Index

W

HOW TO PURCHASE ASTD PRESS PRODUCTS

All ASTD Press titles may be purchased through ASTD's online store at **www.store.astd.org**.

ASTD Press products are available worldwide through various outlets and booksellers. In the United States and Canada, individuals may also purchase titles (print or eBook) from:

Amazon– www.amazon.com (USA); www.amazon.com (CA)
Google Play– play.google.com/store
EBSCO– www.ebscohost.com/ebooks/home

Outside the United States, English-language ASTD Press titles may be purchased through distributors (divided geographically).

United Kingdom, Continental Europe, the Middle East, North Africa, Central Asia, and Latin America:
Eurospan Group
Phone: 44.1767.604.972
Fax: 44.1767.601.640
Email: eurospan@turpin-distribution.com
Web: www.eurospanbookstore.com
For a complete list of countries serviced via Eurospan please visit www.store.astd.org or email publications@astd.org.

South Africa:
Knowledge Resources
Phone: +27(11)880-8540
Fax: +27(11)880-8700/9829
Email: mail@knowres.co.za
Web: http://www.kr.co.za
For a complete list of countries serviced via Knowledge Resources please visit www.store.astd.org or email publications@astd.org.

Nigeria:
Paradise Bookshops
Phone: 08033075133
Email: paradisebookshops@gmail.com
Website: www.paradisebookshops.com

Asia:
Cengage Learning Asia Pte. Ltd.
Email: asia.info@cengage.com
Web: www.cengageasia.com
For a complete list of countries serviced via Cengage Learning please visit www.store.astd.org or email publications@astd.org.

India:
Cengage India Pvt. Ltd.
Phone: 011 43644 1111
Fax: 011 4364 1100
Email: asia.infoindia@cengage.com

For all other countries, customers may send their publication orders directly to ASTD. Please visit: **www.store.astd.org**.